TWAYNE'S WORLD AUTHORS SERIES

A Survey of the World's Literature

Sylvia E. Bowman, Indiana University
GENERAL EDITOR

CANADA

Joseph Jones, University of Texas
EDITOR

Mazo de la Roche

(TWAS 129)

TWAYNE'S WORLD AUTHORS SERIES (TWAS)

The purpose of TWAS is to survey the major writers— novelists, dramatists, historians, poets, philosophers, and critics—of the nations of the world. Among the national literatures covered are those of Australia, Canada, China, Eastern Europe, France, Germany, Greece, India, Italy, Japan, Latin America, New Zealand, Poland, Russia, Scandinavia, Spain, and the African nations, as well as Hebrew, Yiddish, and Latin Classical literatures. This survey is complemented by Twayne's United States Authors Series and English Authors Series.

The intent of each volume in these series is to present a critical-analytical study of the works of the writer; to include biographical and historical material that may be necessary for understanding, appreciation, and critical appraisal of the writer; and to present all material in clear, concise English—but not to vitiate the scholarly content of the work by doing so.

Mazo de la Roche

By GEORGE HENDRICK

University of Illinois

Twayne Publishers, Inc.　:　:　New York

Preface

Who reads Mazo de la Roche? Why have her Jalna novels sold millions of copies? Why were her non-Jalna stories and novels only moderately successful? Just who was this Canadian writer who ground out saga after saga of the Whiteoaks? Just how did she manage to write what the public wanted?

Chapter 1 of this study is a biographical essay recounting the genteel outer world of Mazo de la Roche's Victorian childhood in Canada and the teeming inner world of her Brontë-like Playland. The chapter also suggests some of the emotional bonds she shared with her father and with Caroline Clement, who was to be her life companion. The turmoil of Miss de la Roche's inner world and her observations of life in Canada and England provided the material for her most popular stories and novels.

With *Jalna*, her third novel, Miss de la Roche found the form which a large reading public wanted: a story about a large, diverse, landed-gentry family, whose members included an imperious, aristocratic Grandmother; her sons and daughter; her virile grandson, Renny; her artistic great-grandsons Eden and Wakefield; and dozens more of descendants, wives, husbands, lovers, and neighbors. Miss de la Roche's vivid imagination peopled the tight little world of the Jalna estate with recognizable yet exaggerated characters, and in novel after novel she told the story of the Whiteoaks. Miss de la Roche's publishers clearly wanted her to continue the series, for her books sold well; her readers begged for more stories, for the Whiteoaks became real to them. Miss de la Roche complied; by the end of her life, she had published sixteen novels about the Whiteoaks.

Miss de la Roche invited the millions of housewives who formed a large part of her audience to participate in life at Jalna, in its quiet domestic scenes and in its scandals and upheavals. Her readers could walk through the Jalna woods; visit the barns, stables, and fields; enjoy cozy teas and huge meals; view the drama of disrupted marriages, illegitimate births, forbidden passions.

Miss de la Roche (as did other writers concocting fiction primarily for housewives) created larger-than-life characters with exaggerated passions. Thousands of Miss de la Roche's readers wrote to say that they were entertained by and delighted with her Whiteoaks. The fans spoke of their pleasure in reading the stories; but almost none of them mentioned the scenes of infidelity, incest, and other sexual irregularities often present in the Jalna stories. The housewives who were constantly writing to Miss de la Roche commending her for her refusal to write "trashy" or "sensual" works expressed appreciation to her for writing novels which were proper for their adolescent daughters to read. Either Miss de la Roche's readers were incredibly naïve or they deluded themselves about the situations in the Jalna stories. What the Jalna series shows is that a large public wants entertaining, easy-to-read fiction; the excitement of legal and extra-legal sex without having it called pornography; and a strong story line to fill the void of a boring world.

Some writers such as Harold Robbins, Herman Wouk, and Jacqueline Susann have been accused of deliberately setting out to give the public what it wants to read or thinks it wants to read. Certain book publishers are alleged to be overly interested in profits. *Time*, in inelegant language, has said that Bernard Geis, who published Miss Susann's *The Valley of the Dolls*, "manufactures best sellers frequently by latching on to sexy manuscripts and spending large amounts of money on ballyhoo." [1]

Publicity certainly played a part in Miss de la Roche's first success. *The Atlantic Monthly*, which awarded her a $10,000 prize for Jalna; Little, Brown, and Co., which published the novel in the United States; and Macmillan's, her English publisher, were restrained in their advertising. The paperbound editions in England, brought out by Pan, tended toward flamboyant statements. For the Pan edition of *Whiteoak Harvest*, the editors emblazoned on the back cover the tangled sex problems of Jalnaland: "Jalna in the thirties—Renny and his wife Alayne—their marriage near disaster . . . Finch and Sarah return from their honeymoon to upset the household with Eden Whiteoak's love-child . . . Wakefield engaged to Pauline Lebraux, but tormented by religious doubts . . . A complete and captivating story in its own right, *Whiteoak Harvest* is one of the famous Whiteoak Series—world sales total over twelve million books." The "blurb" effectively states the emotional problems to be encountered in the novel and assures the readers that it is proper to enjoy the continuing Jalna stories—after all, twelve million others had paid for the novels and found escape from their worries in the problems of the Whiteoaks.

It would be much too simple, however—and unfair—to think that Miss de la Roche wrote to exploit deliberately her public's hunger for the merely salacious. From her early childhood, Miss de la Roche dwelt in a Playland which supplied her with overwrought fictional material and kept her an emotional adolescent all her life. The Play had some resemblances to the childhood secret world of the Brontës. The three Brontë sisters, however, gave up the world of Angria and Gondal and proceeded to more mature fiction. Miss de la Roche maintained her adolescent Play, and her literary abilities never matured. The stories Miss de la Roche wrote for *Munsey's Magazine* just after the turn of the twentieth century were written with a particular audience in mind. By the middle 1920's, however, she was presenting in her Jalna fiction, quite apart from the dictates of popular journals, a projection of the Play, of life with a virile man, a strong old woman, sensitive artists, men and women tortured by sex in several varieties.

A product of Canada at the turn of the century, Miss de la Roche presents to the reader recognizable landscapes and Canadian and Empire character types. She also had a streak of frontier humor and a realistic sense of raucous Canadian life, as demonstrated in her second novel, *Delight*. Her early novels, *Possession* and *Delight*, though they have the Play elements, showed her to have latent abilities as a realist. The reading audience and the critics were not enthusiastic about these novels. In later works, she let the Play take over: almost instinctively, it appears, she gave her audience what it wanted. Her public liked the world of the landed gentry in Canada; they liked the smell of the Jalna stable.

Whatever Miss de la Roche's motives for writing what she did, it seems clear that her publishers' understandable wishes for more and more such successes as *Jalna*, together with the poor critical reception of her early attempts at realism and frontier humor, helped to push her into the mold of popular writer. Admittedly, however, it was her superior story telling

ability which held her readers' interest through generation after generation of Whiteoaks.

Chapter 2 is an account of the early fiction; its failure as literature and its failure to gain a wide audience. Chapters 3 and
4 are an account of the Jalna series and the reception of the
novels by critics and fans. Chapter 5 continues the discussion
of Miss de la Roche's non-Jalna fiction, the biographical studies
of her adopted children, her short stories, her romantic history
of Quebec, and her strange autobiography. Miss de la Roche's
attempt to gain recognition with her non-Jalna writing was
doomed to failure by a public which preferred the romantic
and emotional episodes, the larger-than-life characters in the
Jalna series.

If her novels about the Whiteoaks or about her other fictional characters are compared with works of recognized, serious writers of her time—with Henry James, D. H. Lawrence,
Ernest Hemingway, Willa Cather, or William Faulkner—it is
immediately clear that her works can not be judged as "serious."
Indeed, Miss de la Roche should not be seriously compared with
such writers. She was invited by fans and some critics to think
of the Jalna novels in the tradition of John Galsworthy's *Forsyte* Saga, but she herself was perceptive enough to realize that
the Jalna books were important because they were popular.
Their popularity is still high, and the Jalna novels are still in
public and lending libraries and are available in cloth and paper
editions in the United States, Canada, and England. Inexpen-
sively priced translations are often seen in France, Germany,
and many other European countries. The stories of the Whiteoaks obviously will hold many readers for years to come. They
are, therefore, worthy of study.

—GEORGE HENDRICK

University of Illinois,
Urbana

Acknowledgments

This study of Mazo de la Roche as a popular writer was begun in Europe, and I am indebted to Miss A. Sante, Librarian of the Amerika-Institut, Johann Wolfgang Goethe-Universität, Frankfurt/Main, West Germany, for expert help in gathering material. My assistants in Frankfurt, Dr. Armin Frank and Dr. Manfred Triesch, also aided me in the early stages of this study. Librarians in England and America have also extended me many kindnesses: at the British Museum, the Newberry Library, the University of Illinois at Chicago Circle and at Urbana. I particularly want to thank Miss Marion E. Brown and her staff in the Department of Rare Books and Special Collections of the University of Toronto for their help. Macmillan and Company in London allowed me to use their valuable clipping books of reviews of Miss de la Roche's books.

I am also indebted to Mrs. Ellery Sedgwick for permission to quote from Mr. Sedgwick's letter to Miss de la Roche; to Mrs. Virginia Douglas Dawson and Mrs. Betty Douglas Herman for permission to quote from a letter of Lloyd C. Douglas to Miss de la Roche, and to the Executors of the Estate of Miss de la Roche to quote from two letters by Miss de la Roche to her fans.

Pan Books, Ltd., has allowed me to quote from their blurbs on the covers of their paperbound editions of the Jalna Series. All quotations from the Jalna Series in the text of this study are from the Pan editions (except for *Young Renny*, the Pan edition of which was lost in transit to the United States; references to *Young Renny* are to the 1935 American edition). References in the text to the other works of Miss de la Roche are to the English editions. I have attempted to keep footnote references to the minimum by incorporating many page numbers into the text.

Chatelaine granted permission to quote from the synopsis of *I Hear the Thunder of New Wings*.

Alfred A. Knopf, Inc., granted permission to quote from *Explorers of the Dawn*.

Doubleday and Co., Inc., granted permission to quote from *Quebec*.

As indicated in the Selected Bibliography, Miss de la Roche's books were (with a few exceptions) published by Little, Brown, and Co. in Boston and by Macmillan in London.

Little, Brown, and Co., granted permission to quote from the following: *The Building of Jalna, Finch's Fortune, Jalna, Mary Wakefield, The Master of Jalna, Renny's Daughter, Return to Jalna, Ringing the Changes, Variable Winds at Jalna, Wakefield's Course, The Whiteoak Brothers, Whiteoak Harvest, Whiteoak Heritage, Whiteoaks of Jalna, Young Renny, Whiteoaks: A Play*. The following titles have reverted to the author's estate: *Beside a Norman Tower, A Boy in the House, Growth of a Man, Lark Ascending, The Sacred Bullock and Other Stories of Animals, The Thunder of New Wings, The Very House, Portrait of a Dog*; Executors of the Estate of Mazo de la Roche have kindly allowed me to quote from these works. The Executors of the Estate also provided me with the photograph published on the back of the jacket.

Macmillan and Company, Ltd., in London have granted me permission to quote from the following: *Beside a Norman Tower, A Boy in the House, The Building of Jalna, Delight, Finch's Fortune, Growth of a Man, Jalna, Lark Ascending, Mary Wakefield, The Master of Jalna, Possession, Renny's Daughter, Return to Jalna, Ringing the Changes, The Sacred Bullock and Other Stories of Animals, The Two Saplings, Variable Winds at Jalna, The Very House, Wakefield's Course, The Whiteoak Brothers, Whiteoak Harvest, Whiteoak Heritage, Whiteoaks of Jalna, Young Renny, Low Life and Other Plays, Whiteoaks: A Play, Portrait of a Dog, Bill and Coo, The Song of Lambert*.

Hawthorn Books allowed me to quote from Ronald Hambleton's *Mazo de la Roche of Jalna*, a study of the greatest benefit to me. While I may disagree with a few of his specific interpretations, I regard his study to be of great importance, as I noted in my review published in *The University of Toronto Quarterly*, XXXVI (July, 1967), 410-11.

Once again, my greatest indebtedness is to my wife, who worked with me during every stage of this study.

Contents

Chronology

1879   Mazo Roche (later de la Roche) born to William Richmond Roche and Alberta Lundy Roche in Newmarket, Ontario. (Her birthdate is given as 1885 in *Twentieth Century Authors* and other biographical dictionaries.)

1886 (?) Meets Caroline Clement, her cousin, whom she later "adopts" as a sister. They are to spend much of their childhood and all of their adult lives together, to be finally separated in 1961 by the death of Miss de la Roche.

1902   First publication in *Munsey's Magazine*. Suffers serious "nervous breakdown" during her 20's.

1911   Roche family moves to farm near Bronte. Mazo, then 31, had been publishing stories for ten years, but with small success.

1915   Death of father and move from country to Toronto.

1920   Death of mother. Continues with her writing while Caroline does office work to help support them.

1922   Publication of *Explorers of the Dawn*, a collection of stories.

1923   Publication of *Possession*, her first novel.

1925   Production of one-act play, *Low Life;* followed by other one-acters, *Come True*, 1927; and *The Return of the Emigrant*, 1928. All were first produced in Toronto.

1926   Publication of *Delight*, her second novel.

1927   Awarded $10,000 Atlantic-Little, Brown prize for *Jalna*, the first of a long series on the Whiteoak family.

1929   Went abroad for first time. She and Miss Clement lived away from Canada, primarily in England, until 1939, making only occasional visits to their homeland.

1931   Adopted two small children.

1929-   Publications included *Whiteoaks of Jalna*, 1929; *Portrait of a Dog*, 1930; *Finch's Fortune*, 1931; *Lark Ascending*, 1932; *Beside a Norman Tower*, 1932; *The*
1939

Thunder of New Wings, 1932; *The Master of Jalna*, 1933; *Young Renny*, 1935; *Whiteoak Harvest*, 1936; *The Very House*, 1937; *Growth of a Man*, 1938.

1936   Stage production of *Whiteoaks* in London. Production ran for almost three years. The play was also staged in Canada and the United States.

1939-   Returned to Canada at beginning of war. Publica-
1961   tions during these years included *The Sacred Bullock and Other Stories of Animals*, 1939; *Whiteoak Heritage*, 1940; *Wakefield's Course*, 1941; *The Two Saplings*, 1942; *The Building of Jalna*, 1944; *Quebec: Historic Seaport*, 1945; *Return to Jalna*, 1946; *Mary Wakefield*, 1949; *Renny's Daughter*, 1951; *A Boy in the House and Other Stories*, 1952; *Whiteoak Brothers*, 1953; *The Song of Lambert* (juvenile), 1955; *Ringing the Changes* (autobiography), 1957; *Bill and Coo* (juvenile), 1958; *Morning at Jalna*, 1960.

1951   Stage production of *The Mistress of Jalna*.
1961   Died July 12.

CHAPTER 1

Mazo de la Roche:
Life of a Popular Writer

"D E LA ROCHE, MAZO (1885-[1961])," the brief sketch in *Twentieth Century Authors* (1942), begins, "was born in Toronto, the daughter of William Richmond de la Roche and Alberta (Lundv), de la Roche, but spent her childhood on her father's fruit farm in Ontario. She hated the city and loved the country, where, a sensitive, shy, and often lonely child, she grew up among horses, dogs, and other pets. She was educated at home, and was utterly unfitted for city life when her father died and they had to leave the farm and go to Toronto to live. She, her mother, and a cousin who became her adopted sister existed only for summers, when they went to a cottage on a lake deep in the Ontario woods. There she began to write, first plays and then novels."[1] Such an account would lead one to believe that Miss de la Roche's early life was extremely uneventful, one truly of no more interest than a brief paragraph. Ronald Hambleton in his valuable biography *Mazo de la Roche of Jalna* (1966) has shown, however, that the de la Roches were really the Roches, that Miss de la Roche was born not in 1885 but in 1879, and that she was thirty-one when the family moved from Toronto to a fruit farm near Bronte.[2] As will be shown, her early life was not as presented in *Twentieth Century Authors*.

I *The Secret Play: The Beginning of Her Fictional World*

Now that Mr. Hambleton's biography has been published, the early life of Mazo Roche appears more fascinating; and the mysteries and intrigue are heightened when one reads *Ringing the Changes*, her highly eccentric autobiography which might properly have been given the subtitle "Dramatic Stories About My Life." She begins her memoirs with the story of her first meeting with her cousin Caroline, an intensely Victorian account of an encounter fully as emotional as those in the lives or fiction of the Brontës.

The re-creation of the scene surrounding Caroline's arrival at the Roches' is startlingly similar in dramatic description to Heathcliff's coming to Wuthering Heights as a child wrapped in Mr. Earnshaw's greatcoat. Mr. Earnshaw returned home late at night; Hindley and Cathy had been allowed to wait up for him. As their father unwrapped the bundle in his arm, he said: "See here, wife! I was never so beaten with anything in my life; but you must e'en take it as a gift of God; though it's as dark almost as if it came from the devil." [3]

On a snowy January day in Canada, visitors to Miss de la Roche's grandparents brought in a large bundle, "from the top of which now hung, like limp petals of a flower, strands of silvery fair hair." [4] When the shawls were removed, there sat solemn-faced Caroline Clement, dazed by the scene around her. Unlike Heathcliff, however, the young Caroline was angelic. Later, upstairs, the two girls played and talked; and, decades later in her autobiography, Miss de la Roche spoke of the "delicious intimacy" (xiv) between them. The young Mazo had never before had a playmate; now she had found the "perfect one" (xv). The scene is described in purely innocent Victorian terms, with a complete lack of psychological awareness.

The children sat, heads touching, as they read *Through the Looking-Glass;* the January sun was reddening the walls, but Miss de la Roche does not use the color as Miss Brontë uses Heathcliff's dark skin. Reddening walls in Miss de la Roche's scene are merely reddening walls—a colorful touch, nothing else. Passion and violence are not being consciously suggested.

Aunt Eva, an adult interloper, invaded the Lewis Carroll secret world of the children and made them "feel we had been caught doing something naughty" (xv). The children refused to let the aunt into their world; and, when she had gone, Mazo told her secret, a secret never before revealed, a secret which was to be central in the creation of her fiction:

"It was a dream," I said. "First it was a dream—then I played it—all by myself. I play it every day. But now you are here, I'll tell you and we'll play it together."

"What do you call it?" she whispered, as though under the weight of a mystery.

"My play I call it. But now it must be *our* play. We'll play it together —if you think you can."

"I can play anything—if it's pretend," she said decidedly. "I've never tried it but I know I can" (xvi).

In her memoirs, Miss de la Roche remembers that, when she awoke from the original dream, she felt that she had left something of herself "submerged" within it and that she had brought something from the dream which had made her different.[5] When she wrote her autobiography, however, she had long since forgotten the incidents of the dream, though the characters were still alive in her imagination. All of the six characters were boys, children of her own age. She explained this oddity of gender by noting that she had been reading volumes of *Boy's Own Magazine* which belonged to an uncle. Even in 1957, when she published her memoirs, Freudian psychology apparently had no significance for her.

Caroline sat in "the wintry twilight, tiny, fragile, receptive as a crystal goblet held beneath the tap" (38), Miss de la Roche recalled dramatically; and Caroline never forgot the six boys or their appearance, which Mazo described to her in great detail.

This carefully constructed account of the meeting with Caroline, dramatic though it be, is highly suspect. Miss de la Roche almost never mentions dates or ages in her autobiography, but she makes a point of emphasizing that she was seven that January day. Ronald Hambleton in his biography of Miss de la Roche believes the meeting was in 1894.[6] This date may, however, also be in error.

Whatever the age of the two children when they met (Mr. Hambleton does not publish Miss Clement's birth date, but from internal evidence in his book it would appear to be 1882), the Play became the most important thing in their lives. Miss de la Roche remarked in her memoirs, "I believe it is not unusual for children to invent playmates, sometimes grotesque, with which they amuse themselves in lonely hours. The Brontës had an imaginary kingdom. But I would find it hard to believe that characters invented by two children ever survived for so many years" (39).

Miss de la Roche seems to have known of the Angria and

Gondal cycles of the Brontës, and it is most likely that her information was from such a source as Mrs. Gaskell's biography of Charlotte instead of Miss Fannie E. Ratchford's scholarly studies. The Brontës' secret world became ordered when the Reverend Mr. Brontë bought a box of toy soldiers for Branwell. The children each claimed a soldier and named it: Charlotte christened hers the Duke of Wellington; Emily chose a grave-looking one whom she called Gravey; Anne had her Waiting Boy; and Branwell called his Alexander Sneaky, alias Bonaparte. In *The Four Brontës*, with its useful synthesis of previous scholarship, Lawrence and E. M. Hanson have suggested that the Brontë children then "began to lead a double existence in their games."[7] The Hansons have also suggested that the children began with miming but soon gave the game permanence by writing down the stories.[8]

Mrs. Gaskell quotes an important extract from Charlotte's "Tales of the Islanders"—a passage which helps explain the imaginative minds of the children. One stormy night in December of 1827, the children sat in the kitchen of the Hayworth parsonage. They had just quarreled with Tabby, the maid, who would not light a candle. Branwell had declared that he didn't know what to do.

Tabby.—"Wha ya may go t' bed."
Branwell.—"I'd rather do anything than that."
Charlotte.—"Why are you so glum to-night, Tabby? Oh! suppose we had each an island of our own."
Branwell.—"If we had I would choose the Island of Man."
Charlotte.—"And I would choose the Isle of Wight."[9]

Anne and Emily also chose islands; and, before being sent off to bed, the children began to people their island kingdoms with characters. In June, 1828, Charlotte continues, "we erected a school on a fictitious island, which was to contain 1000 children."[10]

The adventures now generally referred to as the Angrian and Gondal cycles began to be written in the now famous miniature books. The Hansons conclude their chapter on "Angria and Gondal" by asserting that the juvenile works of the Brontës can be traced to many sources. "But we must look elsewhere," the Hansons go on, "for the original and co-ordinative element which distinguishes them from the writings of other children.

This is to be found in the Brontë imagination—compact of Irish father, Cornish mother, and Yorkshire environment. And it is this creative imagination, bold, impassioned, richly and unfailingly inventive, which gives their early writings distinction and their novels greatness."[11] Mazo de la Roche did have an over-active imagination, but the terms "distinction" and "greatness" cannot be applied to her fiction.

The young Mazo and Caroline developed the Play, up to a point, along certain lines similar to the Brontës. At first the Canadian children interchanged the six characters, but personality traits of the fictional beings did not develop, and the girls then each took three characters. Caroline does not seem to have brought any leadership into the Play; indeed, Miss de la Roche always refers to herself as the leader. It was she who decided to add women to the cast, the first being a small girl. The girl was a success, and many women characters were invented. As she recalled in her memoirs, "There followed, after a few years, an orgy of new characters. Whenever interest slackened, up, out of my fertile brain, popped another member for the tribe. And such was the unfailing thrill of this, that we almost feverishly avoided the outside world" (39).

Mazo's stories were apparently fertile with elements of violent "orgy" giving the children many hours of surreptitious, feverish, thrilling rapture. When the girls at one time were in the parlor engaged in their Play, Mazo heard her Aunt Eva coming to spy. The passage in Miss de la Roche's memoirs sets the proper emotional tone:

I sprang to my feet, as frightened as though I had been caught in something wicked—fearful that our Play might be stopped. I had, the instant before, been a strong man, gripping the arms of my chair, in a moment of formidable decision. At the movement of the curtain, the sound of Aunt Eva's voice, I became in a flash, a frightened child. . . . Then I heard my father say crossly, "No, I won't spy on them." And Aunt Eva followed him away. . . . I tried to recall what words I had been saying which might have been in that moment overheard. Yes—they were these: "Blount should grip the arms of his chair so hard that his knuckles turn white." And in manly resolution I had, with my small hands, been gripping the arms of my chair. The sweat of humiliation started on my forehead. But Caroline, once the danger was past, showed no perturbation. "Come on," she said, "be

Blount again." And in the darkness we turned once more to the rapture of our Play (40).

This scene is important as a demonstration of the overly emotional playacting of the children, an emotionalism which crept into most of Miss de la Roche's fiction. The scene also shows the great mistrust young Mazo had of the adult world. Ronald Hambleton has argued persuasively that the menacing figure of the spying Aunt Eva was transformed into the spying Mrs. Handsomebody in several stories in *Explorers of the Dawn*. Part of Miss de la Roche's enmity toward Aunt Eva may also be explained by Eva's marrying Pierre Mansbendel, a suitor of sorts of Miss de la Roche. It is clear from the paragraph quoted above that the young Mazo was alienated from the world around her, and that she and Caroline created their own melodramatic version of reality. Mazo was Blount in much of her published fiction.

Obviously, there are important differences between the Angrian and Gondal cycles and the Play. Mazo Roche did not write down her fantasies, but the two girls did remember them, perhaps cling to them, certainly continue them. Miss de la Roche implies in her autobiography, published in 1957, that the Play still engaged the no longer adolescent (at least in age) adoptive sisters. The Brontë sisters, in contrast, gave up their cycles for more mature writing. Miss de la Roche's writing, even when she was past seventy, was essentially that of an adolescent girl caught in a fantasy world.

II *Ancestry and Early Life*

The Play indicates that Miss de la Roche had an active imagination which made it difficult for her to deal with the reality of her family and her early life. She remembered that her relatives were all handsome but that not one had distinguished himself. Having made that admission, she does not in her autobiography explain why she added *de la* to her name. Would an aristocratic name somehow help make a nobody somebody? For any rational discussion of Miss de la Roche's ancestry and for interesting information which helps explain the characters of her parents, one should turn to *Chapter IV* of Hambleton's biography, which separates, as completely as possible, the fact from the fiction of her memoirs.

Miss de la Roche devoted two chapters of her autobiography to her forebears, but the information is highly selective and essentially eccentric. Names and dates were seemingly of little importance to her, though one is drawn more and more to the conclusion that the vagueness was an attempt to hide a great deal of the past. She remembered her maternal Grandfather Lundy as a gay, alert man given to sudden tempers. Suitors of his daughter Eva often were subjected at the dinner table to haughty disdain, and the meal would progress in silence. At times he could be kind, as when Mazo's mother was suffering from one of her numerous nervous collapses. Grandfather Lundy, who was "convinced that the scent of pine, balsam and spruce" would cure her, filled her room with boughs. Miss de la Roche seems to have inherited many of his characteristics; Mr. Hambleton has noted that as an old woman she often made disparaging remarks, in a voice which all could hear, about other diners in a restaurant. Though her Grandfather Lundy was volatile, her grandmother was tranquil. Mazo spent much of her childhood in the Lundy home.

On the paternal side, the influence of her Irish great-grandmother is most important. Sarah D. Bryan (1794-1881?) was charming, but she had a fiery temper; she was demonstrative but domineering. Like the fictional Gran Whiteoaks, she "overbore her children and her children's children" (13). Miss de la Roche hints in her autobiography that her father's family descended from an aristocratic French family. Mr. Hambleton quotes the wedding notice of her paternal grandparents in the *Christian Guardian* for January 10, 1849: John R. Roche "of the county of Limerick, Ireland, late student of Belfast College" to Sarah Bryan. [12] The family seems to have used the name Roche consistently, though one uncle—Francis—did in 1882 sign one of his books "Francis J. de la Roche." He may well have been as romantic as Mazo. One need not discount, however, the possibility of a family belief that the Roches were originally French aristocrats.

Grandfather Roche was a lover of books and bought them extravagantly. According to family legend, he left wife and

[21]

children for better opportunities in the United States. He spent much of his life residing in Baltimore, away from his Canadian family. When he died in 1880, his obituary said he was a professor of mathematics at Newton University. No such institution, Mr. Hambleton has found, existed in Baltimore.[13]

Miss de la Roche in her autobiography says that a son went to Baltimore for the body and returned with it and twenty-eight crates of books, which were to go to the youngest son Francois (Francis, according to Mr. Hambleton, was the uncle who in one of his books signed his name "de la Roche," though he regularly used the name Roche.) The adolescent boy, a lover of books, opened the crates; and in the last one, he later confided to Mazo, he found bundles of letters. They were, he said, "letters from certain ladies of Baltimore. It was not as though they were from only one woman. There were several and they all seemed very much in love with him" (26). He read all the letters and then burnt them to keep others from seeing them. Miss de la Roche's reaction is typical of her Celtic imagination. She kept the story to herself, for her mother "would have been too interested" and her father "would have dismissed the affair with an amused and tolerant smile" (27). Later she introduced a similar scene in the Jalna series. She did not believe in wasting her material.

Mazo's mother, Alberta Lundy, was frail and quiet; her father, William Richmond Roche, was healthy and outgoing. Miss de la Roche in her memoirs said of her parents:

> They had many things in common. Both loved country life, horses and dogs—she in moderation—he to excess. Both were extravagant in dress—for her the most expensive shops—for him, the best tailor. Both—with the best intentions—ran up bills which afterward they found difficult to pay. Both were extravagantly generous to friends and family. Both demonstrative in affection. She quick in anger and retort. He slow to anger, forbearing, but when roused, violent in his rage (12).

Mazo was born, Mr. Hambleton has shown, in the small town of Newmarket, some thirty miles from Toronto, where the Roche family had business interests. Danford, her father's brother, owned a store; and William R., her father, was among other things an independent grocer (the business failed), an employee of a local miller, a store manager, and a traveling salesman.

Miss de la Roche in her memoirs dramatizes her birth scene. Her mother came down with scarlet fever, and labor and the disease undermined her health. When the baby was delivered by Dr. Bradford Patterson, who was married to her great-aunt, the doctor named her for a girl he had once been in love with. Miss de la Roche remembers her early childhood:

> From being a delicate infant I grew into a healthy little girl, much humoured, yet affectionate and biddable. My memory goes back to my very early days. It is an unusual memory that has brought me both pleasure and torment. Seldom have I been able to forget anything. A scene of pain or cruelty which I may have witnessed as a child returns to me to-day with terrific vividness. The first such happening I remember was the sight of a dog, running in terror through the street, with a tin can tied to its tail. There were boys in the street who doubled up in laughter and shouted at him. My astonishment that such a thing could be, my helplessness to prevent it, made an impression that years could not dim (31).

These cruelties outside her home seem to have been extremely troubling to her, but the constant moves of her father from job to job, from house to house, are given almost no attention. In 1882, when Mazo was three, the family moved to Toronto, where Danford enlarged his store in which Mazo's father worked. The William Roches then lived for some time with the Lundys. There, the young Mazo, with her Celtic imagination, was subjected to horrible fears. One of her dreams, inspired in part, one suspects, by *Alice in Wonderland* and in part by universal sexual fears, was this: "In my dream I saw a dim tunnel and, rolling smoothly through it, an enormous ball that almost filled the tunnel. I stood in its way. Nothing could save me. At the same time I heard a distant roaring sound. A strange smell, the very essence of evil, stole through the tunnel. I woke crying and wet with sweat" (32).

It is also clear from the memoirs that Mazo was a bookish child. The elders read to her constantly, it would appear. She owned many books, and was especially fond of Lewis Carroll's *Alice in Wonderland* and *Through the Looking-Glass*; Charles Kingsley's *The Water Babies*; Charlotte Yonge's *The Little Duke* and the Kate Greenaway books. Lewis Carroll seems to have made the greatest literary impression on her. One may well connect the story of the tunnel and Alice's fall down the rabbit hole. Mrs. Florence Lennon, in her provocative but often wrong-headed book *The Life of Lewis Carroll*, has noted, "The fall down the rabbit hole, for instance, is a birth dream indeed —and what a symbol—the Rabbit for fertility!" (152-53). Mrs. Lennon goes on, in her inimitable fashion, "Birth dreams are universal, but since we are born without language, they use visual and muscular imagery; whatever reminds us of birth retains a mysterious fascination, unaccountable till this great discovery of Dr. Rank's. *Wonderland* contains all the elements. . ."(153). Few would wish to believe such a simple Freudian explanation of *Alice in Wonderland*, even though the sexual elements in the story are now widely recognized. Similarly, the sexual elements in Mazo's dream are evident but not easily analyzed.

III   *Early Writings and Juvenile Reading*

Miss de la Roche recalled in her autobiography that, when she was nine, she saw in *The Youth's Companion* a notice of a short-story competition. She set out to win the prize, and wrote an eight-page story about Nancy, a lost child. Fortunately, this bit of juvenilia has not been published, but Miss de la Roche did summarize the story:

> Terrible times she went through but at last was restored to her mother's arms—my own heart ready to burst with emotion as I finished the story with a text from the Prodigal Son.
> "But, darling," said my mother, "do you think a child would ever be so hungry she would eat potato parings?"
> "Nancy was," I said firmly.
> "And do you think her mother would quote a text the moment her child was given back to her? It sounds so pompous."
> This was my first experience of criticism and how it hurt!

Her father defended the story. It is clear, though unstated, that Mazo was becoming more closely attached to her father and more alienated from her mother.

The story was rejected, and Mazo was dejected. The editor replied, "You are very young to have entered the competition but, if the promise shown by this story is fulfilled, you will make a good writer yet" (41). The insensitive mother said, "Isn't that splendid!"—and Mazo broke into sobs. The father, Miss de la Roche recalled, had the good sense to distract her by teaching her how to play cribbage.

Mazo and Caroline attended a private school during the day, but Miss de la Roche remembers learning little, though she read widely. By the time she was ten (one may wish to add a few years), Dickens was a favorite. She went through *Oliver Twist* numerous times but *The Old Curiosity Shop* only once because, interestingly enough, she hated Quilp and found Little Nell's death overly sentimental! When the teacher began to read *Misunderstood* aloud to the class, the reading had to be stopped because Mazo was "overwhelmed" (43). The caricatures and grotesqueries of Dickens clearly influenced her view of the world and of art, and Miss de la Roche's later fiction abounds in Dickensian scenes.

She was, then, a bookish child who read whatever came her way. One of her uncles had been given a copy of *The Adventures of Hadji*, and Mazo read it. Soon afterward, her grandfather, who happened to find the book, promptly consigned it to the fire; for he found the book to be "nasty." Miss de la Roche added humorously in her memoirs: "Little did he dream that the small grand-daughter, standing innocently by, was thanking her stars that she had finished the book before its destruction. I believed Grandpa when he said the book was wicked but I could not believe that it had hurt me to read it. I concluded that what might be harmful to a young man could not hurt a small girl" (43). She continued the Play with Caroline, and she went on reading. Her reading included Maria Louisa Molesworth's *Carrots: Just a Little Boy* and Louisa May Alcott's *Little Women*, though she really preferred *Little Men*. Her reading tastes were rather more masculine than feminine.

From the time she was six, she was taken to the theater. She remembered in her memoirs: ". . . I saw some of the great actors in plays I could not understand and that sometimes frightened me a little but also gave me a strange pleasure" (43). These dramas, acted in the fashion admired by Victorians, undoubtedly contributed to the overly dramatic view of the world she was to present in her own fiction.

When Mazo was eleven (according to Mr. Hambleton, to

whom one must almost always turn for pertinent dates), the Roches moved from Toronto to Galt primarily for the sake of Mrs. Roche's health. She suffered from bronchitis, according to Miss de la Roche in her autobiography; but Ronald Hambleton speculates that Mrs. Roche was probably suffering from severe depression. At any rate, the Roches did not take a house but rented a suite in a hotel and ate in the dining room. The move to new surroundings was one, Mazo recalled, which they all looked forward to with great anticipation. The father was especially endowed with a buoyant nature; and, while Mrs. Roche and Mazo shared this mood at times, Miss de la Roche recalled in her old age that she "had also a dark strain of melancholy. From the heights to the depths has been my Celtic inheritance" (46).

Her anticipation of a new life was so strong that she did not seem to have objected to parting from Caroline. In fact, she remembered writing to her only one time: "Then I wrote to her as one of the characters in our Play. He was a young man named Bernard. In this letter I told her of my fine score at cricket and enclosed a picture of myself in cricketing costume, cut from the *Illustrated London News* —a fine upstanding young man" (46). The masculine role she was assuming was indicative of a growing attachment to her father and of an increasing remoteness from her mother.

The Roches moved with them volumes of Shakespeare, the sets of Dickens and Scott, and Dr. Johnson's dictionary. Mazo continued to spend much of her time reading. In her autobiography she puts down some of the titles: Charles Dickens's *David Copperfield* and *A Tale of Two Cities;* Sir Walter Scott's *Rob Roy* and *Quentin Durward*. These novels no doubt excited her romantic imagination. Her recollection of the reading habits of her parents during the Galt years is also a good indication of Mazo's own feelings about them. She recalled that her mother was not particularly fond of Scott but liked Dickens, the Brontës, Jane Austen, and Rhoda Broughton. Clearly, Mazo was reading the great nineteenth-century novelists (Rhoda Broughton perhaps included), but she does not say so. She does not say she read with her mother. The story is different, however, when she turns to memories of her father. What Miss de la Roche does is to dramatize a love scene:

Often my father and I read the same book at the same time, his six

[26]

foot three extended in an easy chair, my growing length draped against his chest. So I remember reading *The White Company, Harry Lorrequer, Allan Quatermain* by Rider Haggard . . . . I think it was in these days, when first we began to read together that the bond between my father and me strengthened into a deep understanding and we became the most loved of friends. As he waited for my slower grasp of the page to catch up to his, as his large shapely hand was raised to turn the page, a palpable emotion stirred within us (53).

Miss de la Roche interrupted this tender scene in her memoirs to declare that she instinctively loved her mother. Then, obeisances to her mother made, she returned to her father: "As I grew older and young men appeared on the scene, I invariably compared them with him, to their disadvantage—till the day when one arrived who could better bear comparison with him." She never married.

At night the bookish three often recited poetry. Mrs. Roche might declaim Tennyson, purring verses in the wrong order. Mr. Roche recited "The Wreck of the Julie Plante" while Mrs. Roche, Mazo, and the dog were entranced. One night Mazo chose "Jabberwocky" and acted out the lines:

> One, two! One two! And through and through
> The vorpal blade went snicker-snack!

She seized a paperknife, she remembered, and flourished it: "I never knew how it happened, the blade struck the back of my mother's hand and great red drops of blood came spurting out. In consternation, in shock, I threw down the paperknife and bent over her hand. With eyes full of concern for my pain, she cried: 'It's nothing—it didn't hurt at all!' " (54). Mother was long-suffering, and Miss de la Roche does not comment on the scene. Perhaps as an old woman, she still had no understanding of the meaning of the scene she had just dramatized.

The Roches, at the mother's insistence, decided to read Shakespeare aloud to Mazo. In the first play, *Othello,* Papa was to play the Moor, Mama was to be Desdemona, and Mama and Papa divided all the other roles. Mazo and the dog were the audience. During the first performance, Papa read a passage which made Mama recoil in horror. Perhaps it was Iago's speech to Desdemona's father:

> Iago. 'Zounds, sir, you're robb'd! For shame,
> put on your gown.
> Your heart is burst, you lost half your
> soul;
> Even now, now, very now, an old black ram
> Is tupping your white ewe.

Whatever the passage was, Papa Roche insisted that Mazo and the dog wouldn't understand. Mama, Mazo remembered, "cast doubtful looks on both me and the pug, and we, feeling embarrassed, slunk into the next room" (55).

The only other reading of significance she mentions during the Galt years was *Chambers's Historical Questions with Answers*. She was particularly intrigued by the Classical Greek section and became a pagan convert, "worshiping at the shrines of the bad old gods" (60).

Mazo's great friend during the first months in Galt was Mina Sylvester, daughter of a local doctor. Miss de la Roche explains the basis of the friendship: "She was more like Caroline than any other child I had known—the responsive companion, ready to fall in with all my inventions, my imaginings" (50). Mina died of appendicitis during the Roches' first year in Galt, and Mazo does a set piece describing the burial in the forest of one of Mina's trinkets: "I stood for a time motionless among the trees, my forehead pressed against the rough bark of a half-grown pine. Trees were my companions, I felt" (58). But more than the trees remained; Caroline was found again when the family left Galt. And the companionship with trees may have been more derivative than instinctive.

After two years, the family moved back to Toronto, where they lived with Grandfather Lundy. Caroline was also sent to live there, and the two adolescent girls began their Play again:

> Quietly we savoured the joy of being together once more. We did not put our arms about each other's waists, as most girls would; we did not look into each other's eyes; but, gazing at the lake, we talked and talked, and at last, without effort, took up our parts in our Play again. The characters were few, their doings were wildly imagined, but—oh, the fascination of it! (67).

Caroline was a shy, attractive girl by then; and, since her tastes were similar to those of Mrs. Roche, the two spent much

[28]

time together. Although it is unsaid in this section of the memoirs, Mazo was still undoubtedly much more strongly drawn to her father. The two girls led quiet lives; Caroline was too delicate to attend regular school and took private lessons. Although the girls led completely sheltered lives in their Grandfather Lundy's house, they did begin to have boyfriends, though Victorian formalities made these young courtships difficult. As Miss de la Roche commented: ". . . we and our friends talked not at all of sex or marriage as a reality, though we were enthralled by it in romantic fiction and the theatre. The reason. . . was that the times were hard. There was little money in the hands of young men. Their salaries were too small for the support of a family" (73). One of her boyfriends introduced her to the works of Henry James, Gissing, Arnold Bennett. Art could safely take the place of sex in Victorian times.

During these adolescent years (just *when* Miss de la Roche does not specify in her memoirs), she began to write plays. The young Mazo and Caroline had been much taken with romantic stories such as Sir Anthony Hope Hawkins's *The Prisoner of Zenda*, Richard Harding Davis's *Princess Aline*, and Rudyard Kipling's *The Light that Failed*. They often went to the theater, where they saw everything from Charles Hawtrey's *The Private Secretary* to Oscar Wilde's *Lady Windemere's Fan* and Alexandre Dumas's *Camille*. Mazo's first play (for family and friends) was *A Passage at Arms*. She took the role of a cavalier, and Caroline played the innkeeper's daughter.

Several such romantic plays followed. As Miss de la Roche recalled: "That one-act play of mine was the first of a number I wrote, always for a cast of two. Almost always Caroline was the heroine and I the hero. Always were the costumes picturesque. The most successful was one in which I was a gypsy fortune-teller. The scene was in Spain during the Napoleonic wars" (75). These plays were probably not much worse than the typical Hollywood romantic-historic dramas of the 1920's. They also indicate that Mazo was not outgrowing the masculine role and that her inner dramatic world excluded all others except Caroline.

Caroline and Mazo spent all their available time with the Play. When Mazo should have been studying, Caroline would come in, and they would begin their drama. The early Brontë

stories were often amoral, and Miss de la Roche said of her
creations: "These characters were not yet loved by us for their
qualities. Often they were cruel. Their adventures were ill-
considered. We were in no way bound by time but would pass
over a year in no more than a minute. The various parts were
interchangeable, so that a character would be bandied back and
forth, acted differently, as Shylock by different actors is differently portrayed" (77).

IV *Adolescent Suffering*

The Play also had practical value. Mrs. Roche suffered from
attacks of nerves, and she could not stay in the house during
one part of her life unless there was a man in it. Since Mr.
Lundy and Mr. Roche were often away, one of Mr. Roche's
elderly relatives, Uncle Bryan, was invited to live with them.
Just hearing him about the house was enough to soothe Mrs.
Roche. On one occasion, however, Uncle Bryan had to be away
at the same time all the other men of the house were on trips.
Mazo was afraid his absence "might mean the snapping of
that slender cord that bound her [mother] to reason." The Victorian, Brontëan, Dickensian, slightly decadent scene followed:

Suddenly an inspiration came to me. I would be the instrument to
save my mother from fear. . . In Uncle Bryan's bedroom I found a
pair of his boots. I put them on and creaked heavily down the stairs,
along the passage, past my mother's door, and down the other stairs to
the hall below. . . The deception worked. Thereafter, several times a
day, I mounted and descended the stairs, wearing my great-uncle's
boots, even, in my girl's voice, forced a deep "ha!" from my throat as
I creaked along the passage (80).

Troubled by her mother's instability, Mazo became even more
miserable when Caroline fell in love with Roderigo, a young
man from South America. Mazo, reacting in hurt, felt as if
Caroline "had broken some unspoken pact" (83). The affair was
soon broken off, for there were family objections: he was a
Catholic. After Roderigo left, Mazo could not understand Caroline's grief. They chased their pain away by returning to the
Play. For the first time, she says, the characters "took on a new
significance. Their relations with each other became more intense. The passing of time too became controlled. No longer

would we hasten through a year in a few days or anchor a loved character to a desired age. Two of them had remained at fourteen and fifteen years, regardless of passing time" (85). One is tempted to speculate that the two characters who had remained the same age were Mazo and Caroline; they were fastened into perpetual adolescence.

During this time of intense Play activity, they became even more involved in the action. When one of the characters met a violent death, the grief-stricken girls resurrected him. They never again killed off a fictional creation, for, she says, "there was quite enough of suffering in our own lives" (86). This statement might well stand as a part of her artistic credo, for in most of her novels she offers escape; the reality of suffering and pain are glossed over.

Grandfather Lundy died in 1900 when Mazo was twenty-one, and the family broke apart. Mr. Roche had a succession of jobs for the next few years, and the family again moved from one house to another. During this time, Mazo was beginning to write seriously. The setting of her first story, published in 1902, was French Canada, a section of the country she knew little about; but she had her everactive imagination. This first story, taken by *Munsey's*, pandered to the reading public. This story and others set in the mythical hamlet of St. Loo are discussed in Chapter 2.

In her memoirs, when speaking of these first stories, she expressed part of her artistic creed: ". . . imaginative writing is one of the most delightful of occupations. It is exacting, it often is exhausting. It demands everything the writer has in him to give. He must believe in the characters if he is to persuade the public to believe in them. What the writer of fiction needs—first, last, and all the time—is a public. Its interest is the steady wind that fans the fire of his creative ability" (95-96). From this statement it is apparent that, even as a beginning writer, she was greatly concerned with her audience. Excessive interest in what the public wanted to read was one reason she never developed into a serious writer.

Not long after the turn of the century—if the autobiography can be trusted—Mazo had a serious nervous breakdown. As she recounted it, she learned by accident that she had failed to include return postage with a story she thought to be her best.

[31]

What was thought to be a lost manuscript became an obsession. Perhaps seeking a miracle—the return of her manuscript—she went into the Catholic Cathedral and knelt at each Station of the Cross. Defiantly, she told her family what she had done, and then took to her bed. For weeks she remained there, smothered in self-pity. Caroline, who slept with her, soothed her. Mazo complained to an uncle, "I'm going to die—like Grandpa died" (104). Fear of death—not the loss of the manuscript—was undoubtedly a large part of what was troubling her.

She was finally taken to the country, where she began to improve. Caroline went away for a short visit—perhaps that departure helped relieve some tensions—and Mrs. Roche read Charlotte Brontë's *Villette*, Emily Brontë's *Wuthering Heights*, and R. D. Blackmore's *Lorna Doone* to her. Not surprisingly, elements from these novels appeared in her own fiction; she heard them at a time when her imagination undoubtedly made much of the action and mood. For three years her health was precarious, and she was unable to write: "Nearly a year passed before I was able to write a letter. In truth I look back on the three succeeding years with a feeling of confusion. I can barely recall the times when I thought it might be possible for me to write. . ."(107).

The Play continued in those years, but she says that it "became more subtle. Now one sentence might be more pregnant than formerly a complete episode had been. My physical strength was not equal to the force of my teeming imagination. I could write so little without strain to the nerves that our Play became the outlet. My written stories were mere cups that were inadequate to contain the stream. The capacity of our Play was boundless" (116). Her imaginary world and the one of her Art (if one can use the word) are here well described. The statement helps to explain the final failure of her stories and novels.

V Country Life

The world of Miss de la Roche's autobiography was timeless. Suddenly one finds the family ready to be farmers, ready to take to country life on a fruit farm near Bronte, on Lake Ontario. Mr. Hambleton reminds one, contrary to the account in

Twentieth Century Authors, that she was then over thirty, but the tone of the autobiography leads one to believe she was perhaps fifteen or sixteen. Mr. Hambleton also reveals in some detail what is only sketched in her memoirs: the Roches, acting the part of gentlemen farmers, were doomed to financial failure.

Miss de la Roche and Miss Clement (naturally she went along) each had projects—Miss de la Roche raised chickens. Mr. Hambleton has found a marvelous, unintentionally comic interview with Miss de la Roche, published in the *Toronto Star Weekly* on February 7, 1914. Even the title is hilarious—"Joan of the Barnyard—A Young Poetess Who Loves Chickens." Katherine Hale, the interviewer, began by announcing that Miss de la Roche was gaining attention for stories published in American magazines. Miss Hale's description of Bronte makes it appear as desolate as the Haworth of the Brontës, but Miss Hale was too busy linking Miss de la Roche with chickens to think of connecting the name Bronte with Charlotte, Emily, and Anne.

The talk of the interview was unliterary and apparently authentic:

"Look at that wonderful face," said the girl, as we stood before the stall of a big beautiful Jersey. "Do you know any human with such sympathy and such silence in her eyes? These animals make one rather dislike talking to people. When I am much in town, I come back with a clearer conviction that words don't mean anything at all. The chickens are, of course, unlovable as types, fighting, restless bits of temperament, but they are so heartless and so dramatic, so compelling in their own brief way that you cannot help being interested" (104).

During the latter years on the farm Miss de la Roche met Pierre Mansbendel. They were attracted to each other; but when she hesitated, he married the hated Aunt Eva. Miss de la Roche did not feel his loss too greatly then. Her closest attachment was still to her father, and her great loss during these years was not Pierre but her father, who died in 1915. His death occurred not long after the family had been forced to leave the unprofitable farm for an apartment in a nearby house, an apartment which is the setting for the curious novelette *A Boy in the House.*

[33]

VI *Toronto, again, and the First Novels*

The three women began to make plans to return to Toronto. Before their departure from the country, Miss de la Roche began to write the stories later collected in *Explorers of the Dawn*. When they were again settled in the city, Miss Clement took a civil service position; and Miss de la Roche stayed at home and concentrated on her writing.

The three and their dog or dogs led quiet lives. Miss de la Roche began to join literary clubs. Her stories were appearing with some regularity. In 1920, Mrs. Roche died. The lives of Miss de la Roche, Miss Clement, and the dogs continued to be quiet. During the summer they went to the country, where, finally, they bought land and had a cottage built. Dorothy Livesay in "The Making of Jalna: A Reminiscence" has recalled that the two adoptive sisters retreated to Trail Cottage because Miss de la Roche would be undisturbed there. Miss Livesay remembers that Miss Clement commuted to Toronto during the summer, leaving Miss de la Roche free to write all day. "In the evening," she goes on, "after supper with her half-sister, Mazo would read aloud what she had written that day. If Miss Clement approved, the chapter was allowed to stay in the book."

The 1920's—until 1927, at least—were placid. *Explorers of the Dawn* was published by the prestigious Knopf firm. Miss de la Roche began to think of writing one-act plays and a novel. The first of her novels was *Possession* (1923). The second was *The Thunder of New Wings*, rejected by her publishers, but finally printed in 1932. Her third novel, *Delight*, which was written in the comic vein, was less a commercial success than the first novel. All of these novels are discussed in Chapter 2.

VII Jalna

After the mixed reviews of *Delight*, Miss de la Roche turned to a novel she had begun in 1925. "Two of the characters," she says, " . . . had been half-formed some years earlier and were to have been characters in a play that never was written. They had no names but later they were to emerge as Meg and Renny Whiteoak . . . " (181). The manuscript of this new novel was sent to Macmillan's of New York, but she later saw in the *At-*

lantic Monthly notice of a novel competition. Though tied to a Macmillan contract, she also entered the contest.

Edward Weeks, who was a young editor in 1927, remembers in his book *In Friendly Candor* the details of the Atlantic contest. Over a thousand novels were submitted, and they were rejected at the rate of eighty a day. First readers did the initial screening for the editors. A librarian first reader made these comments on the manuscript of *Jalna:* "This is the story of a large love-making family in Canada, dominated by the old grandmother. The brothers have unseemly affairs with their sisters-in-law, and there is quite a lot about the stable, including the odor. Not recommended" (85). When Weeks began reading *Jalna,* he was entranced; and other editors also approved the stable odors.

Ellery Sedgwick, editor of the *Atlantic Monthly,* sent this private and confidential note to Miss de la Roche on March 26, 1927: "I congratulate you from my heart. I have known your struggles for twelve, or has it been fourteen years. At any rate, I have doubts of the lengths of your dresses when you first wrote, but now I have no doubt of your maturity, your intuition of character, or your imagination. You have won the prize." But, contrary to Mr. Sedgwick's expectations, Miss de la Roche did not mature as a writer. She was almost fifty when she had her first great success, but her girlish imagination remained just that. It was perhaps unfortunate for the development of her literary talent that she won the prize. Pressures from entranced readers and profit-seeking publishers made her repeat her story time after time, as will be shown in Chapters 3 and 4.

The difficulty of having two publishers for the same book was worked out. Macmillan published the book in Canada and Atlantic-Little, Brown in the United States. When news of her $10,000 prize became known, Miss de la Roche was a celebrity. Miss Livesay has captured the feeling of those who knew her: "We all wept for joy. It was not merely that a Canadian writer had been recognized in the United States, it was not merely that we felt that Mazo de la Roche's work deserved recognition, but it was also the fact that she who had been really poor would now be able to write without the gnawing fear of poverty." [14]

Canadians had not been accustomed to having acclaimed, well-paid authors in their midst. Every club and civic organization wanted to honor her. Even as she approached fifty, she was still girlishly shy; and when she and Miss Clement fled the publicity, her seclusion made her even more of a celebrity.

Miss de la Roche cringed from much of the publicity but learned to endure the tortures of public meetings. Her mind turned, however, to a sequel to *Jalna;* and in 1928, after Miss Clement gave up her civil service position, the two sailed for Europe. They first stayed in Sicily before going to England. It was apparently during the Mediterranean part of their trip that the two Canadian spinsters met a tubercular English artist, his pregnant wife, and their small daughter. After the two ladies had departed for England, the artist died from a hemorrhage and his wife died in childbirth. Not long afterwards, Miss de la Roche adopted their two children.

VIII   *Life in England*

The years 1929-1939 were spent mostly in England. Undoubtedly Miss de la Roche wanted the kind of aristocratic life she could live there, and she now had the money to rent a series of cottages and houses. When the children came to her in 1931, she added a nursemaid, and soon hers was almost a baronial life, with cooks, servants, governesses. She was living an even more exalted life than the one she was extolling in sequel after sequel of the Jalna story.

Miss de la Roche and Miss Clement had some literary contacts (with J. B. Priestley and Hugh Walpole, for example), but they obviously preferred English social life. While Miss de la Roche went on writing of her imaginary Whiteoak family, she apparently experienced the happiest years of her life. She now had children, money, dogs, Miss Clement, friendly publishers, devoted readers. She knew that she had readers waiting for each new account of the Whiteoaks. She could move from one large house to another, and Miss Clement was always there to supervise the decorating, to listen to the latest chapter, to be an Alice B. Toklas. At last, Miss de la Roche had the gracious life appropriate to her name. In her autobiography, these years take a disproportionate amount of space; she was still writing of the romance of life, and hers was a fairy tale come true.

During these years she wrote six Whiteoak novels. Two times she tried to develop other subjects—*Lark Ascending* (1932) and a *Bildungsroman* entitled *Growth of a Man* (1938). Both were artistic failures. Both were largely ignored by her readers: the public wanted more of Jalna. She had more success with her nonfiction; the account of Bunty in *Portrait of a Dog* commanded a large audience of dog lovers, and the two accounts of her children—*Beside a Norman Tower* (1932) and *The Very House* (1937)—were sentimental enough to appeal to many women readers.

Perhaps the greatest excitement of these years was the production of her play *Whiteoaks*, which opened in London in 1936 and ran for almost three years. Such a dramatization had seemed a natural development since the publication of *Jalna* in 1927. In 1933 she had begun serious work on an adaptation, which, after many revisions, was produced three years later. Ronald Hambleton has recorded the history of the production, and one should consult his excellent account for the details. The adaptation reintroduced her to the theatrical world (her one-act plays of the 1920's were produced by amateur groups) and, more importantly, brought her work to the attention of a somewhat different audience. Undoubtedly the play helped the sales of her novels. The play is discussed in Chapter 3.

IX *Last Years in Canada*

The last years of her life—1939-1961—are ignored in the autobiography. She moved her family back to Canada at the beginning of the war. She remarked, cryptically, in her autobiography: "And there for years I lived and wrote quite a number of books . . . . This latest period of mine is mostly a record of books written, of seeing a different sort of world rise into my astonished view" (303-304). Ten of the novels of this period were about Jalna. Of the two others, only *A Boy in the House* (1952) is of real interest.

These years were apparently unpleasant for her. Advancing age, poor health, loss of readers to television were all troublesome. Fortunately, Miss Clement remained as faithful as ever. The adopted children married, and there were grandchildren to please her. She had said in her fiction what she had to say, and she kept repeating it. Her imagination kept on working, but it seemed rather tired. She became less and less seen. Canadians did not take her seriously as a writer. Nobody took her work seriously except schoolgirls of all ages, shut-ins, and incurable romantics. They kept on reading her—and she kept on writing for them until the very end of her life.

CHAPTER 2

The Early Fiction

IT is particularly fitting that Miss de la Roche's first major
publications were in *Munsey's Magazine*. Frank Munsey's
journal, which began in 1889, was an immediate success because
of its price—ten cents—and because of the rather risqué pictures which it printed during its early years. Circulation rose to
over half a million, though some readers had doubts that it was
a "family magazine," and the public library in Wilkes-Barre
canceled its subscription "because of the many illustrations . . .
which are of the nude order."[1]

Munsey did publish stories and serials by such writers as F.
Marion Crawford, James Oliver Curwood, Clarence Budington
Kelland, O. Henry, and others more easily forgotten. Clearly,
the fiction was meant for the popular reader. Frank Luther
Mott has observed that, though *Munsey's* was not a first-class
magazine, it had a large circulation and made substantial profits. "It did this," he states, by publishing "light but rather unori-
ginal writing."[2]

I St. Loo Stories

By the time Miss de la Roche published in *Munsey's*, risqué
pictures were no longer a staple and the magazine was conventional. Her first story to be published there, "The Thief of St.
Loo: An Incident in the Life of Antoine O'Neil, Honest Man,"
which appeared in the November, 1902, issue, was part of an
aborted series of stories set in St. Loo, a mythical village in
Quebec and Playland. It was a sentimental story, praising conventional religion; but its setting in a rather obscure corner of

Canada gave it a small amount of "local color." It was exactly the mediocre fiction *Munsey's* readers wanted.

The story was an account of the young Antoine O'Neil who needed fifty cents to buy beads for twelve year-old Margot, his "dearest friend," to wear to her confirmation. The relationship of the two, as befits a Victorian story, was sexless. The boy himself was sexless; his aunt had been fearful to trust him with the men in the lumber camp and had kept him at home with her. He was, however, a frequenter of Remi Leduc's tavern, where he enjoyed the gaiety and the music.

When Antoine told Remi of his need for money, the tavern keeper suggested he win the change from the drunken Jean Ratte. The money was soon Antoine's and he bought the necklace from a storekeeper and rushed to the girl's house, where he saw her through her window. She was praying before the crucifix, and he was so shamed at spying on her while she was with the saints (a Hamlet echo) that he returned the necklace and traded it for potatoes which he delivered to the Ratte family. He was again an honest man. The story ended with a moral tag. Returning home, he found on the road a frozen sparrow: " 'Poor little bird,' he whispered to it against his cheek, 'you will sing no more, but the heart of Antoine will sing forever, because he is honest man, him!' " (187).

The second St. Loo story to appear in *Munsey's*—"The Son of a Miser: How Noel Caron, of St. Loo, Proved That He Was No Pinchpenny" (published in the August, 1903, issue)—was no better than the first. Noel, the miller's son, is first seen counting his father's hoarded fortune. The miller had just died, and the curé had advised the boy not to lay up treasures on earth. In an overly dramatic, Dickensian scene, the boy counted the $5,000 in hoarded money, drinking brandy all the time. The brandy was a Sure Sign—the boy was headed for Victorian Trouble. He was determined not to be a miser; he would buy beautiful things for the beautiful Laure. But he discovered she did not want bangles, that she was practical and did not wish to throw money, even miser's money, away. "I do it," he said, "but to right myself." (Obviously this was a line from the Play.) Her reply is in perfect keeping with his dramatic statement: "I am to be made a doll, then, in order that St. Loo shall lie? Don't speak to me" (754).

Naturally, the boy went on a debauch, spent money on a common girl, bought fancy clothes, fell in with evil companions, and drank. His money was soon gone, fortunately, before he was beyond redemption. Out of money, now down and out, the boy discovered a worker in the mill who wanted to buy his property and to marry Laure. The boy came to his senses in typical form, appeared at church on Easter, not in finery but in his clothes of six months before. His jacket would hardly fit him, for he had matured, was now a man. One of Miss de la Roche's sexual images then follows: "His long limbs protruded from his garments most uncouthly" (756). (Fifty years later, she was still blundering into such images.) Uncouth as he was, he planted all his finery on the chancel steps and begged forgiveness. The curé forgave him. Laure left the church, and he met her at a roadside Calvary, with red branches of cherry tree over the head of Jesus. Laure was kneeling, naturally. He took her hand. She forgave him.

Miss de la Roche had again written what the readers thought they wanted. After all, the boy was not *very* wicked. He *did* confess his sins. He did win the girl. Victorian values were not critically examined.

Another St. Loo story—"The Spirit of the Dance" (appearing in the May, 1910, issue of *The Canadian Magazine*)—was a more developed and more romantic story. It began as Dr. Giraud came to the Seigneur's house on a professional call. The old Madame Berthe was persuaded to tell a long story about the present Seigneur, M. Louis. She had been in the household over forty years and had known the present Seigneur since his birth. As a young boy, he had loved music. A poetic child, he could hear poplars whispering to him. He was a fine violinist and was sent away to Montreal to study music. When he returned, she liked his playing less—it was colder. Then he went to Rome to study, and there a Roman lady gave him a Stradivarius. He married her, and returned home in four years, leaving his wife there but bringing home his child Gabrielle.

The old housekeeper kept hearing weird music at night—sounding as if it were a "dance of dead leaves in November"—and finally she peeked through the keyhole and saw Gabrielle dancing to the Seigneur's music. When the girl came out of the room, Tante screamed at her and called her evil. The girl explained that her father had told her to dance; the next day, the Seigneur was enervated. The old woman thought the music was an evil and that the girl had no power to resist. When the doctor went into the Master's bedroom, M. Louis admitted that "It's the music madness that is killing me." The violin was taken away from him and sold to the innkeeper for money to buy nourishing food for M. Louis, who was sending every cent he had to his wife in Rome.

When Gabrielle was awakened some time later by her father, who needed music, she ran down the road to the tavern and borrowed the Stradivarius; she then sped home, changed into her nightgown, and, barefoot, danced for her father. The scene which follows is obviously a sexual one. She danced; she "threw herself with graceful force from posture to posture, her white limbs bathed in moonlight. Then as the music grew wilder, she became only a part of the harmonious whole, like the waving poplar and the singing violin" (47). She danced in shadow and in moonlight, and laughter "babbled from her lips." Louis played on, his whole soul poured out: "It was a supreme moment. They both realized it, and as their eyes met once, they exchanged glances of admiration and delight as the dance proceeded" (48). The dance of love completed, "the melody trailed off. . . .The breeze fell, leaving the curtains limp and white against the window where the poplar tree stood motionless with an expectant air" (48). When the girl looked again at her father, his "soul. . .had gone out into the night" (48).

Much of the sexual imagery in the last scene foreshadows Miss de la Roche's later use of erotic materials in the Jalna series. Had this story been filmed in the 1920's, it would now be a "camp" favorite. The St. Loo stories, which sound as if they were direct transcriptions from materials acted out in the Play, are of interest to the modern critic only because they indicate the state of popular taste at the turn of the century.

II   Explorers of the Dawn

Just after the death of Mr. Roche in 1915 and before the three ladies moved to Toronto, Miss de la Roche wrote a story which was the first in a series collected as *Explorers of the Dawn*. Several other stories, all interconnected, were taken by

magazines before the collection was published by Alfred A.
Knopf in 1922. These stories, also seemingly transcriptions of
the Play, were in general more artistically presented than the
St. Loo stories.

The setting is an adolescent's view of a cathedral town in
England. There is the same childish distrust of the adult world
which has been observed in Miss de la Roche's own life. The
semi-ogre of the stories is Mrs. Handsomebody, who spies on
children as Aunt Eva spied on Mazo and Caroline. By the time
these stories were written, Aunt Eva had married Pierre; the
characterization of Mrs. Handsomebody might well be an expression of Miss de la Roche's need for revenge.

The main characters of the stories are the three young Cur-
zon children—Angel (David), nine; John, eight; and the Seraph
(Alexander), five. The point-of-view character is John; and, in
the tradition of the Play, Miss de la Roche takes the male role.
Christopher Morley in his foreword to the volume, points out
some of the unreal qualities of the boys: "I must admit that it
is evident the author of the book was never herself a small
boy: sometimes their imperfections are a little too perfect, too
femininely and romantically conceived, to make me feel one
of them. They have not quite the rowdy actuality of Mr. Tar-
kington's urchins. But the fact that the whole story is told with
a poet's imagination, and viewed through a golden cloud of
fancy, gives us countervailing beauties that a strictly natural-
istic treatment would miss" (11-12).

The boys, untouched by the recent death of their mother,
went from one adventure to another; and they continually
foiled Mrs. Handsomebody, who could only pack them off to
bed without their dinner when they were naughty. The children
did not learn from their experiences. Like Little Orphan Annie,
they were perpetually frozen in their attitudes and in their
emotional age.

It is not quite clear just for what audience the stories were
intended. Since two of the stories appeared originally in *Atlantic Monthly* and three in *Woman's Home Companion*, both author and editors must have thought they would appeal to adults.
Christopher Morley agreed, ending his foreword with this rather curious paragraph: "And so one wishes good fortune to this
book in its task—which every book must face for itself—of

discovering its destined friends. There will be some readers, I think, who will look through it as through an open window, into a land of clear gusty winds and March sunshine and volleying church bells on Sunday mornings, into a land of terrible contradictions, a land whose emigrés look back to it tenderly, yet without too poignant regret—the Almost Forgotten Land of childhood" (13).

Forty-five years have proven Mr. Morley wrong. A modern adult reader might be slightly amused by the caricatures: the menacing Mrs. Handsomebody, the eccentric Bishop in gaiters, the archeologist pretending to be a pirate, the show girl married to a nobleman; he might similarly be amused by the sometime droll sayings of the children; but he is not likely to be transported into the "Almost Forgotten Land of childhood." If the book has any appeal now, it would be to a youthful audience; the stories do read better than the Bobbsey Twins or Nancy Drew stories.

The first story in the collection—"Buried Treasure"—indicates some of Miss de la Roche's strengths in writing popular stories. The children, who had recently lost their mother, had been placed in the care of Mrs. Handsomebody, while the father was in South America building bridges. On Saturdays, when Mrs. Handsomebody went to market, the children were no longer under restraint and could cavort with the Irish maid, Mary Ellen. She is in the popular fictional tradition of the comic maid and never breaks out of that stereotype. One Saturday the four saw next door a strange old gentleman; and, when the boys talked to him, he convinced them he was a pirate. The children were true believers, especially when old Mr. Pegg said part of the buried treasure was in Mrs. Handsomebody's garden. When the three boys and the reformed pirate met late at night to dig for the treasure, they were interrupted, after they had found the chest, by the younger Mr. and Mrs. Pegg and Mrs. Handsomebody. When Mrs. Pegg blurted out that the old gentleman had really buried the chest for the children, Mr. Pegg and Pirate Pegg quieted her. The children, curiously enough, were still believers; and the author did not allow them to understand the revelation.

Mrs. Handsomebody was uncomprehending and spoke of the

treasure as "rubbish." The moral is clear: adults such as Mrs. Handsomebody are not to be trusted. Most literature for children, including *Alice in Wonderland,* has traded on such distrust. The story still has some charm; adults are ridiculous enough to interest children and adults, the language is felicitous, and readers are offered escape into a childhood they wish they had lived.

A few of the stories, notably "The Jilt," are comic. Little Jane, the Bishop's great-niece, offered to make John the father of the doll Dorothea. John even decided to take wife and child to South America with him while he built bridges over canyons. Eternally feminine, Jane gurgled, "I can keep house and hang my washing 'cross the canyon to dry!" Mary Ellen, the Irish maid, explained to John what love is like: "ye burns in yer insides till ye feel like ye had a furnace blazin' there. Thin whin it seems ye must bust wid the flarin' av it, ye suddintly turns cowld as ice, an' yer sowl do shrivil up wid fear." John took on all the symptoms.

When Angel also fell in love with Jane, the two boys fought over her, only to be separated by Mary Ellen, who declaimed "There ain't a lady livin' that's worth messin' up yer clane clothes for" (71). Jane, however, not content with two of the brothers, vamped the Seraph. She said to him: "Say some more drefful things, Seraph. I jus' love to hear you." When he said "Blood" blandly, she shrieked with ecstacy. Angel and John, spying, understood: "It was gore then, that this delicately nurtured young person craved, good red gore, and plenty of it!" (74).

The lesson was not learned by the two older boys; in the later stories they were completely innocent creatures. And the story, for all of its humor, never quite explores the horror of the games children play. The story hints at being a perceptive serio-comic story, but it does not succeed because Miss de la Roche did not discipline her fancy. A comparison of this story with, for example, Katherine Anne Porter's "The Downward Path to Wisdom" demonstrates the pedestrian qualities of Miss de la Roche's story.

"D'ye Ken John Peel?" indicates Miss de la Roche's fatal weakness for the melodramatic and sentimental; it shows no progress beyond her stories set in St. Loo. The boys met Harry,

[45]

a poor young man, and John learned that Harry was the Bishop's "bad" son.

Harry's faults were not serious. He was not a murderer or a rapist or an extortionist. He was wayward though, and his "sins" were small, readily understood and condoned by the readers of women's magazines. The boys conspired to bring home the prodigal son. It is a story well suited to *Woman's Home Companion* readers. Alas, several other stories in the collection are no better.

Explorers of the Dawn was well received by the critics and sold widely. Reprinted the first year of publication, it was on the best-seller list in 1923. Ronald Hambleton has astutely observed that "in *Explorers of the Dawn* there are no emotions, only feelings; no symbols, only counters, with arbitrary, regional, and topical, rather than universal, values" (184). The Play was undisciplined, and these stories share this fault. Miss de la Roche's later fiction was not really to mature significantly, but her predominantly lower middle-class audience had been taught to believe in, and wanted to believe in, the naïve dream world which she presented in this fiction—a world of high-spirited, lovable, innocent children; comic maids; and prodigal sons.

III   Possession

The year after *Explorers of the Dawn* appeared, Miss de la Roche published *Possession*, a novel more obviously intended for adults. She broke her contract with Knopf and gave her first novel to Macmillan's of New York. For subject matter she reached back to her years on the Rochedale fruit farm near Bronte. The mood she wished to re-create was that of Emily Brontë's *Wuthering Heights*. One finds the same loving descriptions of the landscape; a bleakness startlingly reminiscent of the Brontës' moors; the same tortured emotions; a similar tangled love affair; and, perhaps most importantly, a Byronic hero descended from Heathcliff.

The story opens with the coming to Grimstone of Derek Vale, who had inherited the fruit farm from an uncle. Derek found at the farm workers, male and female, and a rather frightening housekeeper, Mrs. Mackin. Derek soon fell in love with Grace, beautiful blonde daughter of Mr. Jerrold, the local squire. Many of the details were obviously strongly autobiographic: Grace had many of the physical traits of Miss Clements, and Mr. Jerrold had many of the qualities (including business failure) of Mr. Roche. One is tempted to speculate that Miss de la Roche again, as in the Play, gave herself the primary male role—Derek.

The early parts of the novel are filled with an odd mixture of romantic landscape description and realistic observations of an Ontario fruit farm. The realism is strengthened with the arrival of the Indian fruit pickers, Chief Solomon and his family. Derek was particularly taken by "dark-eyed little girls," and in these pre-Lolita times he found they made him "feel weakly good-humored, almost helpless." He stole to the lake shore (characters in Miss de la Roche's stories are always spying) to watch the nude bathing: "One of the girls raised her arms to her head to fasten the long wet hair that had fallen about her shoulders. Derek's heart gave a sudden leap; a hot thrill of pleasure stirred, like a pain, in his breast. She seemed to rise, a dark water-lily on its stem, a flower of unearthly beauty, . . ." (52). Derek was as erotically caught up as Whitman's persona watching the twenty-eight nude bathers.

The young Indian maiden, Derek soon discovered, was named Fawnie. Amidst the details of running a fruit farm, Miss de la Roche tossed in a seduction. Fawnie was lonesome and wanted Derek to take her on the lake in his canoe. She guided him to a sheltered cave she knew. The scene itself is not specific but suggestive; Miss de la Roche relied on her readers to add the necessary details. The scene is only five lines long: "The two stood in silence for a moment enveloped in the languorous darkness . . . . 'Fawnie!' he cried low. He felt her soft mouth under his; he was overcome by a sort of giddiness, and, at the same time filled by an immense compassion for her . . ." (74).

This scene out of the way, Miss de la Roche had nine months to fill; for in Victorian fiction a tender encounter almost invariably produces a child. Miss de la Roche couldn't just skip that much time; Edmund, Derek's brother, came for a visit and promptly fell in love with Grace. The next year the Indians returned and insisted that Derek marry Fawnie, who now has had the baby. The Rector recommended holy matrimony; Derek

[47]

suspected that the minister wanted to marry Grace himself. Derek saw Grace in her carriage, but she did not stop to speak to him. His fate was sealed; he decided to marry Fawnie.

In the next section, Derek became a Byronic hero manqué. He took to drink. After the wedding, Mr. Jerrold called to report that the marriage should not have taken place. Grace, he explained, had been upset; she had driven on, then turned back to look for Derek. He could not be found. (The scene is reminiscent of the Heathcliff-Cathy misunderstanding in *Wuthering Heights*). Derek drank more and more. He gambled with the Indians. He let the fruit rot.

Instead of depths of characterization and understanding, Miss de la Roche took the easy way out; she multiplied characters and heightened scenes. For example, Edmund returned hoping to marry Grace; but, Gentle Readers, Grace was in love with her father first and then with Derek; therefore, she would not have Edmund. Moreover, Fawnie ran away with another Indian, leaving the child Buckskin with Derek. And, in a chapter called "Love Among the Hummocks," Derek explained to Grace that he needed Fawnie sexually and Grace platonically. At least, that is probably what he meant: "There's Fawnie, too . . . I was thinking once about a flower—a sort of lily . . . . Its roots are in the mud, its stalk and leaves in the dark water, but its flower opens in the pure air, and turns to the sun and breeze. Well, that's like my love for you. It's the flower of me" (263).

For some reason, in a chapter indelicately titled "Buckskin Strikes His Tent," the author let Fawnie's boy die of a convulsion. When Fawnie reappeared the day of the funeral, she was ill and needed Derek. She was dark and passionate, in a way that D. H. Lawrence understood. Blonde Grace and her father were outside the house but unable to see in the bedroom when Derek got abed. "Derek turned to Fawnie. He put his arms about her, and laid his face beside hers on the pillow" (289). And so the novel ends.

Just before Derek went upstairs to Fawnie in the bedroom, Derek had thought the moral of this novel: He loved his farm now that his own flesh was a part of it, and he loved weak Fawnie: "What a strange thing possession was! You thought you were the possessor when, in truth you were the thing possessed"

(288). The moral tag had been hastily added to a novel which is moral only in outward appearances.

It is indeed curious that the Canadian reviewers in 1923 praised the novel extravagantly, and that the English and American ones were also kind.[3] Four decades after its publication, *Possession* has a rather grotesque flavor about it. The superimposing of Brontë Gothic upon Bronte, Ontario, is more than a little ludicrous.

IV   The Thunder of New Wings

After *Possession* was completed, Miss de la Roche began work on *The Thunder of New Wings*. Her hopes for it were high, as she told the story in her memoirs: "My visit to a certain foggy, out-of-the-way spot in Nova Scotia had inspired it . . . . Nothing I ever had written would equal it. Assuredly nothing I have written can compare with it in failure and disappointment. But—when for the first time I re-read it, this summer, thirty years later, I thought it a remarkable book. Yet I saw where I had gone terribly wrong" (166). Her analysis of what was wrong demonstrates how incapable she was of critical judgment: she felt she had put into it too much " 'guidebookish' description" (167).

When the novel was submitted to Hugh Eayrs of Macmillan in Toronto, he recommended that it be rewritten. Instead, Miss de la Roche put it aside; but in 1932-1933 she allowed it to be serialized in *Chatelaine*, the Canadian magazine for women. According to Mr. Hambleton, her publishers were distressed that the "fiasco" (as Miss Clement called it) was being printed; but Miss de la Roche wrote in a 1931 letter quoted by Hambleton: "I do not think that the serialization of the earlier book can blacken my reputation as my publishers seem to think. For my own part, I like the book and I was rather pleased that it should see the light" (154).

Chatelaine published a synopsis with later chapters of the novel. Each synopsis had a certain charm, for it indicated much about the literary tastes of the readers of the magazine: plot was all-important to them. They did not feel cheated if they bought a copy of *Chatelaine* at the news stand and found the novel in progress. The synopsis gave them all the details they needed to relish the chapter at hand The Synopsis quoted here lays the plot bare, and exposes the patent absurdity of the story:

When Sir Richard Lashbrook died in England, he left a strangely incongruous group of people behind. There were his two daughters, Vicky and Theo—attractive girls in their late twenties, and his second wife, Clara. Ayrton, the son of his second marriage with Clara, and Joan, his niece, who had come from Canada to live with her uncle, completed the little group.

There was a strong feeling of enmity between Clara and her step-daughters. So intense was this dislike that although Sir Richard had provided that his daughters should live at home as long as they wanted to, the three girls, Vicky, Theo and Joan, preferred to cut adrift, and went to live in Nova Scotia on a farm which Sir Richard had owned on the Bay of Fundy. There they encountered strange folk in the sinister Captain Alonzo Haight, tenant of the farm; mystery in the hidden origin of the attractive, graceless young Tobias Haight, adopted son of the captain; and, for Vicky, love in the person of Pat Baldry, youthful mayor of the town.

When Alonzo Haight's insolence and cruelty forced the girls to give him notice to leave the farm, he produced evidence to prove that his so-called son was in reality Sir Richard Lashbrook's son by his marriage to a young French-Canadian girl. Toby was, therefore, the rightful heir to the Lashbrook estates, then in the hands of the girls' hated stepmother. Seeing in Toby a heaven-sent instrument of revenge, Vicky accepted Pat Baldry's offer of marraige, and with Pat, Theo and Joan, took Toby back to England, to oust Clara and her son Ayrton from their home.

Now, back in Cornwall, the girls try to settle into their old lives once more. But the atmosphere of the house is charged with suppressed venom. It is as if all within these walls had been uprooted and thrown together again in undignified confusion, no one where he belonged, to take root again as best they might. Clara persists in remaining with Ayrton in her old home, silently accepting, after her first tortured amazement, the new order of things. Vicky, to the exclusion of her husband, is wrapped with vindictive hatred for her stepmother, and ambition for her young protegé. Toby slips into his position as head of the ill-assorted household with surprising ease.

In chapters seven and eight, Pat left Vicky; Toby fell in love with Clara, one of those semi-incestuous relationships which intrigued Miss de la Roche in her later novels. Toby also invited his "father" and Mr. Teg, an ancient old man given to biblical

[50]

quotations, for a visit. In a boating accident, Toby, Vicky, and Theo were drowned. Two years later, when Joan met Pat again, they were free to be married.

The romantic Brontë elements are obvious: the gypsy-like, not-quite-evil boy Toby, the mystery of Toby's birth, the villain manqué Alonzo Haight who brutally beat Toby in the early section of the novel (a scene reminiscent of the cruelty scenes of Charlotte Brontë's *Jane Eyre*), the impassioned love scenes. All are in the Romantic tradition, filtered through the Play of Miss de la Roche and therefore more adolescent. Characters pop in and out of the action, for no good reason; characters change character, for no good reason. Captain Haight is first evil, then is redeemed. Scenes in Nova Scotia and Devon are improbable, just as the action and the characters are unbelievable. The plot summary effectively shows all these faults of the novel.

When Miss de la Roche reread her novel, she thought it would make a fine movie. But she chose the wrong medium; the novel could have become a successful radio or television serial. As a novel, *The Thunder of New Wings* is not much worse, however, than most of her other fiction. It could hardly have harmed her reputation, for there is every reason to believe *Chatelaine* readers were pleased. When *Chatelaine* editors in October of 1932 spoke of it as "one of the important novels of the year" (30), the readers almost assuredly believed them.

V Delight

The novel *Delight* (1926) grew out of stories told to Miss de la Roche by the family cook at Rochedale. In June, 1911, Miss de la Roche published in *The Metropolitan* a story, "Canadian Ida and English Nell," which was to become, fifteen years later, part of the novel. The book was generally disliked in Canada and had a mixed reception in the United States. For all of its excesses, however, *Delight* is perhaps the best of Miss de la Roche. It is a boldly comic novel set on the Canadian frontier. The comedy is earthy, unsophisticated, and filled with sexual innuendoes. It clearly demonstrates Miss de la Roche's command of frontier humor. Miss de la Roche felt it was far better than the reviews deemed it to be; for she remarked in her memoirs, "To say that it was disliked by some Canadian reviewers is to put it mildly. One Toronto critic in particular was so violent that his review was almost a classic in abuse" (180).

Mr. Hambleton has located the Toronto review to which Miss de la Roche objected. The *Saturday Night* reviewer was offended by two passages, which he could not quote but for which he did give the pages. The offending passages were undoubtedly these: "Her chemise, drawn upward, disclosed her strong, white thighs, glistening in the lamplight" and "her breasts, rising and falling, lay like sleeping flowers beneath her rounded arms." Miss de la Roche was rightly distressed by the review, and in a letter quoted by Mr. Hambleton, she cried out: "Pity the Canadian novelist who does not write of the Woolly West or sweet 'homey' tales" (172).

The novel began on two suggestive notes. Two new servants arrived at the Duke of York. One, Delight Mainprize (the 1920's version of James Bond's Pussy Galore) was exceedingly beautiful; and Kirke, who carried her belongings upstairs, rushed to his room and described her to his roommate. She had, he said, "a red-hot look in the eyes" and his blood was atingle. He admitted, however, that he aspired to marry someone of a higher station. Miss de la Roche is hinting at the double standard which was also prevalent on the frontier.

Upstairs, another suggestive scene was played out. May, the other girl, admitted that she was married to Albert Masters, who had come to Canada before her. He was living in this very town, but May was afraid he had taken up with a Canadian girl. Delight soothed her: "She lay supine in Delight's arms. The girl still rhythmically patted her back" (19). The sexual elements of the scene are heightened when Delight thinks: "It must be awful to be married" (20). Delight, for all her beauty, constantly attempted to escape men; but they yearned for her and continued to make advances.

When Delight waited on tables the next morning, she looked for May's husband; and, finding a young man who fitted the description, she whispered to him, "Remember your May." But Delight had whispered to Jimmy Sykes, not Albert Masters. Jimmy lingered after breakfast; he thought she had said, "Remember, you may." The easy morals of these working people were clearly stated. "I thought you meant I might make love to you," Jimmy said; and Delight agreed to go out with him.

When May found that Albert didn't live at the inn any more, she decided to watch for him in the bar; and she discovered a closet off the bar, where she could see the drinkers. When she saw her husband, she called him into the closet and found he had remarried. Another sexual scene is then described: "They sat in silence now, two little cockney animals that had crept into this dark burrow out of the storm. His lips sought hers. He stroked her cheek. Like a solemn threnody the voices in the bar surged over them. They might have been at the bottom of the sea" (41). The situation of the bigamist husband and the compliant first wife is believable, and the erotic scene is a natural outgrowth of the situation.

When May returned to her room, Delight was unwrapping the apple-green tea set which had been her grandmother's. The tea spout was still intact. (Miss de la Roche may not have read Freud by 1926, but she knew instinctively about tea spouts.) May had agreed to pose as Albert's cousin; she said she would have promised anything in the cubbyhole, for "'E reely is charmin.'" May didn't need to know about tea spouts: she understood the real thing and had no need for symbols.

The most suggestive scene of the novel then follows, but none of the reviewers appeared to have understood it. For the firemen's ball, Delight decided she needed long earrings; but her ears were not pierced, and she could not do it herself. She went to Jimmy's room and asked him to use a threaded needle, place a cork behind the ear, and push the needle through. Jimmy managed to do one ear but became ill and could not do the other. He cried that it was unreasonable and unnatural. When Kirke heard the crying and found both Jimmy and Delight crying, he pierced her ear. The sexual motif is strengthened when Delight said Jimmy was too tender. Kirke said (Hollywood would have had Clark Gable read the line, Rhett Butler fashion), "Well, a tender man's no good to you" (59).

Miss de la Roche also succeeded in showing the sexual implications of dancing. Delight was conscious of Jimmy's body as they danced, as he guided her caressingly. With Kirke, and his "hard" hand, she could dance the Scottish reel. Miss de la Roche caught the right spirit of the country dance, the excitement, the yearning of male and female.

The next scene is boldly comic. May, jealous of Delight's popularity, attacked her friend; and, in their tussle, May's false teeth were broken. It was a tragedy because Albert's second wife was coming for a call that week. May must wrap her face with cloth and announce a terrible toothache. This low comedy scene, typical of frontier humor, is a good example of Miss de la Roche's mastery of that genre. Had the reviewers praised this novel, she might have continued to develop this aspect of her talents, but she was driven instead to the safer and more profitable Jalna stories.

Delight became a great success at the inn, for her beauty drew customers, and the word spread that she was a loose woman. Miss de la Roche then presented a mock-seduction scene. One stormy night, after Jimmy had discovered Delight had had a proposal from a local businessman, Delight and Jimmy tussled and her blouse was torn. She went crying to Bastien, manager of the inn. Kirke had seen what had occurred and, as a practical joke, told the housekeeper, Mrs. Jessop, who was enamored of Bastien. The housekeeper burst into Bastien's room, saw the torn dress, imagined a seduction, and ordered Delight off the premises.

Delight ran away to a fruit farm, where she was lonely and unhappy. She unpacked her teapot thinking of her grandmother who had, in the past, drained "the last drop from its curly spout. . . . " Delight, who could not bear to part with the pot that night, put it on the other pillow, next to the wall: "It would be company, a bedfellow, almost." She got in beside it. Miss de la Roche here leaves nothing to the imagination: "It really was company in this lonely place. She laid one warm hand on its shiny fluted belly. Its spout curved toward her parted lips. She thought: 'I am so happy I cannot sleep,' and in a moment, she slept" (167).

The ending is a complete battle of sexes. The women of the town, led by Mrs. Jessop, lured Delight to the lagoon, where they whirled around her, tore at her clothes, and began ducking her. The men of the town rushed to the lagoon. As they started to swim to the rescue, the women pelted Delight. Mrs. Jessop promised to refrain from drowning the girl if anyone would marry her. And Jimmy won the girl. The men and women, who held no grudges, wandered hand and hand into the forest. "Faint cries were uttered." Sex conquered all.

Desmond Pacey in *Literary History of Canada* has written that the novel is "lively." He finds, however, that "it has little psychological depth; its philosophy of primitivism is not deeply considered; it has no claim to social realism; its style is frequently coy and artificial. It is, in short, a romantic tale whose chief value is as entertainment for an idle afternoon." These faults are certainly there, but they seem less important if one sees the novel in the tradition of frontier humor.

VI *One-Act Plays*

In the 1920's, Miss de la Roche turned to writing one-act plays. Three of them—*Low Life* (1925), *Come True* (1927), and *The Return of the Emigrant* (1928)—were given amateur productions in Canada. *Low Life,* the only interesting play of the group, was, Miss de la Roche says in her memoirs, told to her by a charwoman; but Miss de la Roche added her own touches, mostly from the adolescent Play. One of the characters, Linton, had the air of a fallen gentleman, though, in truth, he had not had far to fall. He had attached himself to Benn, unemployed, and Mrs. Benn, a charwoman, eating their food and taking their daughter's cot. Mrs. Benn had, the day before the play opened, put him out; but he returned during her absence, ate from their scant food supply, and wrote his name on the steam-covered window. When Mrs. Benn returned, she was angry when she saw Linton's name; but he returned and sweet-talked her, saying he was teaching grand manners to their daughter. When Mr. Benn chimed in, Linton was allowed to stay. The psychological problem is an interesting one: Why did she allow him to stay for many months? Why did her husband want Linton, with his airs, in the house? But these questions are not explored.

There were Gothic elements, reminiscent of *Wuthering Heights*, in the play, but Miss de la Roche did not use them. She merely named a character Linton and left her audience to make whatever associations it wished. This play was supposedly a comic melodrama, a slice of down-and-out life with empha-

[55]

sis on humorous dialogue; but the humor seems artificial and out of keeping in the dingy room of the Benns.

Miss de la Roche told a fanciful story in her memoirs about submitting the play for two different prizes and winning both. One group wanted the prize money back, but she had already spent it. Mr. Hambleton showed that Miss de la Roche embroidered the story: she returned the prize money to the Imperial Order Daughters of the Empire, but they declined it. Mr. Hambleton rightly concluded that she wanted to present herself in her memoirs as "naughty and incorrigible" (11).

If *Low Life* was without substance, *Come True* was without any redeeming value. It was set in an old men's home, a Grand Hotel Poorhouse, whose senile old men were given comic lines. One inmate who had inherited ten thousand pounds from a brother, discovered that his ex-sweetheart was in the adjoining old women's home and made plans to marry her. Because the lines in the play are embarrassingly false, it is surprising that even amateurs agreed to produce the play.

The Return of the Emigrant was a short play of thirty-four pages with enough themes to fill a three-act play. There were only three characters: Mary, Maggie, and Kirsteen. The setting was a peasant's cabin in the south of Ireland. Maggie Noland's husband had died ten years before; she was now a somewhat battered woman of thirty-six, and her daughter Kirsteen was eighteen. The play began as Kirsteen entered with three eggs bought to celebrate the return of Mary, who had been in America for twenty years. Mary had not married; at first she worked too hard to pay attention to men, and she was saving her money for her return to Ireland. When Mary entered, she was disdainful of the poverty of her sister. When she told them about the fine foods and the workable plumbing of the Americans, Kirsteen wanted to hear more and more. Mary wanted to end her life with her family, but Kirsteen wanted to marry Johnny and go to America with him. At first the mother wanted to blame Mary for the girl's plans, but Kirsteen, determined to leave, said to her aunt, "It's a rare comfort to me that she'll have you beside her when I am gone." She left and Mary said: "Oh, the darkness—the quiet—the ceiling pressing down. . . . Oh—(She threw out her arms in a tragic gesture.)

I wish it was me that was going out, to the great new land—a little immigrant girl. . . . I wish it was me!" (107).

The play is derivative. Its language is that of the stage Irish, its plotting and mood more important than the characterizations, for Mary, Maggie, and Kirsteen are never more than "flat" characters. The theme of clashing American-European cultures is not really given the treatment it deserves.

Miss de la Roche's early short stories, novels, and plays failed to win her either financial security or popular or critical acclaim. Two of her early novels—*Possession* and *Delight*—showed her to be a writer of some talent, one who was searching for form but never able to discipline a juvenile, romantic imagination.

CHAPTER 3

Jalnaland

MISS de la Roche's early stories often dealt with those who led mean existences. Her inclinations, though, were toward a life of ease and gentility; and her imagination tended toward a glorification of the landed gentry. After her disappointment with the critical reception of *Delight*, she turned again to the Play world of two characters who became Meg and Renny Whiteoak of the Jalna series.

Miss de la Roche's account of the background of the first novel in this series is informative: "Jalna was inspired ,by the traditions of that part of Southern Ontario on the fringe of which we had built Trail Cottage. The descendants of the retired military and naval officers who had settled there stoutly clung to British traditions. No house in particular was pictured; no family portrayed. From the very first the characters created themselves. They leaped from my imagination and from memories of my own family. The grandmother, Adeline Whiteoak, refused to remain a minor character but arrogantly, supported on either side by a son, marched to the centre of the stage" (181).

As usual with Miss de la Roche's accounts, at least part of this one is fanciful. The British gentry tradition in Ontario is real enough, but Miss de la Roche apparently did have a house in mind. Mr. Hambleton prints on page 151 of his biography two splendid pictures of "Benares" which served as a model. Dorothy Livesay in "The Making of Jalna: A Reminiscence" has confirmed Mr. Hambleton's identification of "Benares" (28). Miss de la Roche's autobiography provides ample evidence that she drew details and characters from her relatives. For instance, the portrait of Grandmother Whiteoak owes much to

Miss de la Roche's great-grandmother Bryan. Miss de la Roche knew well the Canadian countryside within a thirty-mile radius of Toronto, as Mr. Hambleton has admirably shown; and she used this countryside as the backdrop for her fiction.

Miss de la Roche's first summer of work on the novel, at Trail Cottage, was one of complete absorption. As she remarked in her memoirs: "In fancy I opened the door of Jalna, passed inside, listened to what was going on"(182). Later, when she was writing the first sequel, her feelings had deepened: "These Whiteoaks. . .now came to be on a different footing with me. I had found them an interesting, a colourful family. Their doings had fascinated me. Now they possessed me. I was one with Finch, for he and I had much in common. I was (at times) one with Renny, for he and I had much in common. At other times I was against him. Never have I been completely at one with any female characters of mine. I might love them, suffer with them, but always they were they and I was I. The closest to me were the two Adelines" (200). This identification with male characters, especially the artistic Finch, is a characteristic already noted in her earlier works. Such identification helps to explain much of the sexual confusion in both her early and late work.

Since *Jalna* contains virtually everything which was included in the later novels, a detailed analysis of it illuminates the entire series. Desmond Pacey in *Literary History of Canada* has provided some outlines for an analysis: he argues that Miss de la Roche should not be considered a social realist and that one should view her as "a romantic writer who set out to communicate an imaginary world of her own creation, and who had the skill and patience to make the real world share her vision." He asserts that, while this estimate may limit her accomplishments, it also clearly defines her literary talents and places her work among the great popular achievements of its time (669).

Professor Pacey also argues convincingly that *Jalna* is at best an entertaining, not a great, novel. He especially praises its "liveliness" and the character delineation. He continues, "Miss de la Roche had learnt from Dickens how to fix a character in our minds by attaching to it a few strong identifying gestures, mannerisms, or habits of speech" (672). He also commends her description of the house and its grounds, but he finds the style "too precious for our austere modern taste." But Miss de la Roche was not writing for "our austere modern taste"; her audience was one that much admired ornate style. Her readers were obviously entertained by the novel's appeal to snobbery, its romanticism, its erotic scenes, and its titillating incidents. All of these help to explain the popularity of *Jalna* and the novels which followed it.

I Jalna

Jalna began with a genealogical chart listing the twenty-or-so members of the Whiteoak family who were to be prominent characters in the novel, plus a few often-referred-to deceased members. Given this large cast of characters, the story inevitably moves ponderously. Using the same episodic structure employed in *Explorers of the Dawn, Possession,* and *Delight*, Miss de la Roche now placed less emphasis on plot. In fact, *Jalna* has little action except for the rather bizarre sex life of the characters. A skeleton of the action shows this: The sprawling Whiteoak family was ruled by a matriarch, Adeline. Piers, an Agricultural Whiteoak, eloped with Pheasant Vaughn, Illegitimate Daughter of a neighbor who had once been engaged to Meg, Big Sister Whiteoak. Much family discussion followed. Eden, the Poet Whiteoak, married an apparently frigid Alayne, and there was more family discussion. Renny, Master of Jalna, fell in love with Alayne; Eden had an affair with Pheasant; there was a great family outburst. Meg married Pheasant's father, and Grandmother celebrated her one-hundredth birthday.

Thus baldly stated, the novel seems a combination of the old radio serial *One Man's Family* and of *Peyton Place*. Since the outside world does not really intrude on the Whiteoaks, the scandal of their lives is heightened. There is great stress on family tradition and a justification of Anglo-Saxon snobbery. The Whiteoaks are praised inordinately, both for their strengths and for their weaknesses. Though their sexual activities are as plentiful and fanciful as those of the lower classes on the fringes of their lives, the Whiteoak family scandal assumes respectability. The Whiteoaks are, after all, landed gentry; and one is not allowed to forget that the Grandmother's family had been related to an Earl. Still, one must agree with Professor Pacey's analysis of the character of Grandmother Whiteoak: "Blunt, coarse, greedy, rude, extravagant, sensual and selfish, she. . .earns the reader's grudging affection by her immense vitality, her insatiable appetite for experience" (672).

The novel begins with a fine chapter on the impish, malingering, scoundrelly Wakefield, not quite ten years old, on his way to lessons. The descriptions are poetic and ring true. But the second chapter is an expository account of the Whiteoaks, emphasizing their gentry traditions, military life in India, the move of the Grandparents to Canada, the taking of land, and the building of Jalna, an imposing structure, the greatest house in the neighborhood. The novel is in fact, a glorification of much the same life, lacking only slaves, that Margaret Mitchell pictured in the beginning of *Gone With the Wind*. As befits such a legend, Captain Whiteoak was handsome; his wife was imperious and headstrong.

In keeping with English domestic drama, Miss de la Roche has many of the scenes played out at dinner or at teatime. Conversations run on rather interminably, for each member at the table or fireside is talkative and is put through his paces, performing in a highly predictable fashion, once one has grasped (and one does so easily) the character's personality.

The imagination of the author takes her into strange byways. One of these bizarre scenes occurs after Eden had brought his bride home to Jalna. Wakefield, a supposedly sickly child, needed constant attention and slept with his half-brother Renny. Unable to get to sleep, Wakefield suggested that they pretend they were somebody else, namely Eden and Alayne, with Renny taking the role of Alayne:

Renny spoke sweetly: "Do you love me, Eden?"
Wake chuckled, then answered, seriously: "Oh, heaps. I'll buy you anything you want. What would you like?"
"I'd like a limousine, and an electric toaster, and—a feather boa."
"I'll get them all first thing in the morning. Is there anything else you'd like, my girl?"
"M—yes. I'd like to go to sleep."
"Now, see here, you can't," objected the pseudo-groom. "Ladies don't pop straight off to sleep like that" (129).

[62]

Was Miss de la Roche merely writing a comic scene? Was she conscious of the sexual overtones of her work? Was she attempting a satire on wedding nights? Was she writing a parody? One doubts that these questions can be answered in the affirmative. More likely her attempt at comedy, though it approaches the edge of sick humor, was merely the outpouring of the same repressions which bubbled forth from the Play.

Another example of Miss de la Roche's strange imaginative byways is Finch's reaction to Alayne (and one should remember that Finch is the character Miss de la Roche is most "at one" with):

His mind dwelt on the thought of kissing the mouth of Eden's wife. He was submerged in an abyss of dreaming. . . . A second self, white and wraithlike, glided from his breast and floated before him in a pale greenish ether. . . . Now it moved face downward like one swimming, and another dim shape floated beside it. . . . One, he knew, belonged to him . . . , but the other . . . whence came it? Had it risen from the body of the girl in the drawing-room below, torn from her by the distraught questing of his own soul? (130-131).

The dim, wraithlike shape of the romantic dream is appropriate for Finch, a teenage schoolboy destined to be a romantic artist in the nineteenth-century grand manner.

Finch discovered Pheasant and Eden together in the woods. (Discovered lovers seemed to have some special significance for Miss de la Roche; she used almost this same scene in *Lark Ascending*. She may have used it, however, not for its psychological significance, but because it was in the romantic mode.) Coming home at night, Finch came to a spot where he had once seen Renny "standing with a strange woman in his arms" (240). At the same spot, he heard low voices and crept in to see what was happening; but, instead of seeing, he heard laughing and the sound of kisses. He knew from the voices who they were, knew they were wicked, knew they were betraying his brother Piers. He rushed to Piers with this dramatic version of the scene: "In the wood—making love—both of them—kissing—making love—" (241). The scene in the woods and the report is intended to titillate the readers, to make them re-create the scene in their own minds.

The love affair between Renny and Alayne was equally passionate but ultimately more socially acceptable. The account of their declaration of love for each other is horsy, in odor and in imagery. Eden, Alayne, and Renny drove into town together. In the tearoom, Eden remarked that Renny smelled "most horribly horsy" and speculated: "I believe you dream o'nights of a wild mane whipping your face, and a pair of dainty hoofs pawing your chest. What a bedfellow, eh, brother Renny?" (189). Eden conveniently had to spend the night in town; and, on the return trip to Jalna, Renny stopped briefly to see a friend. While he was out of the car, Alayne's thoughts kept turning to Renny: "Her mind was becoming like a hound, always running, panting, on the scent of Renny—Renny, Reynard the Fox" (191). Readers of *True Confessions* would instantly recognize what was to follow.

Upon Renny's return to the car, he declared, "if you weren't the wife of Eden, I should ask you to be my mistress" (192). Alayne was willing enough. Miss de la Roche then attempted a poetic description of their ecstasy: "Life in a dark full tide was flowing all about them. Up the lane it swept, as between the banks of a river. They were afloat on it, two leaves that had come together and were caught" (192). Readers of the late 1920's did not need D. H. Lawrence's explicit language to know what was happening, but Miss de la Roche could not resist returning to her horsy imagery: "He, who had all his life ridden desire as a galloping horse, now took for granted that in this deepest love he had known he must keep the whip hand of desire" (193). Miss de la Roche was discrete in presenting this family scandal, perhaps intending all along to let her handsome, virile, strong-smelling hero marry Alayne.

As the novel ends, the imperious old Grandmother—she with the Court nose and ribald parrot who swears in Hindi—celebrates her one-hundredth birthday. The narrative technique as Miss de la Roche explored the thoughts of the Grandmother at that celebration is entirely conventional, as are the thoughts ascribed to her:

One hundred years old! She was frightened suddenly by the stupendousness of her achievement. . . . Beneath her the solid earth, which had borne her up so long, swayed with her, as though it would like to throw her off into space. She blinked. She fumbled for something, she knew not what. She was frightened.

She made a gurgling sound. . . . She gathered her wits about her. "Somebody," she said, thickly, "somebody kiss me—quick!" (268-69).

Those who would admire the worst in Dickens would approve the Grandmother's last statement. Miss de la Roche filled her sixteen volumes of Jalna stories with dozens of such Dickensian scenes.

Clearly, Little, Brown and Company knew what it was doing when it ordered an initial printing of forty-five thousand copies of the novel in October, 1927. The publicity of the $10,000 prize and the heavy advertising of the novel made it inevitable that sales were approaching one hundred thousand by Christmas of 1927. Miss de la Roche and her publishers had a magnificent money machine in their possession.

II   Whiteoaks of Jalna

With money flowing in and with an audience clamoring for more about the virile Canadian gentry, Miss de la Roche turned to a sequel, *Whiteoaks of Jalna*, a name chosen to announce her intentions to her readers of carrying on with the comings and goings of her imaginary family—and the emphasis must be clearly placed on *family*, for one seeking social history would be sorely disappointed. This second novel, published in 1929, contained all of the excesses of *Jalna*. The Grandmother was killed off in a Victorian set piece. Eden, in best nineteenth-century tradition suffered from tuberculosis but was nursed back to health by his estranged wife. As soon as he was able to get about, he ran off with Meg's servant. Alayne was then free to divorce her poet husband and to marry the Master of the House, Renny. Finch inherited the Grandmother's fortune, was abused by the family, and attempted suicide.

Pan Books in 1960 knew exactly how to advertise the novel. The "blurb" on the back cover captured the right tone and substance to lure readers: "Young Finch Whiteoak, callow and thwarted, found the tough life of Jalna a torture he could bear no longer—and tried escape. This is the story, too, of love, of how chance brought back to Jalna the girl whom Renny had once possessed and remembered always—with a passion, forbidden yet smouldering, he knew he could never conquer!"

Perhaps working on the assumption that heterosexual affairs

[65]

were not engrossing enough for her audience, Miss de la Roche
added a touch of homosexuality to the tangled love lives of the
Whiteoaks. Arthur Leigh, an artistic young man, "wanted very
much to gain Finch's confidence, even his love. He felt extraor-
dinarily drawn to the boy . . . " (60). Although Miss de la Roche
was presenting a rather daring subject for 1929, actually nothing much happens, certainly nothing more than what is
shown in this note: "Dearest Finch—After you were gone last
night, I was very much disturbed. You were preoccupied—not
like your old self with me. Cannot you tell me what is wrong? It
would be a terrible thing to me if the clarity of our relationship were clouded. Write to me, darling Finch. Arthur" (116).
Renny, one of the readers of the note, referred to the relationship as a "neurotic affair." Apparently every reader was to
understand what was meant, but Miss de la Roche exonerated
the Whiteoaks: Finch was actually infatuated with Arthur's
sister. Having introduced homosexuality, Miss de la Roche then
dropped the subject. Perhaps she recognized the dangers of it
and did not wish to alienate the more conventional-minded
readers in her audience.

The set piece of *Whiteoaks of Jalna* was the death of the
Grandmother. Having celebrated her one-hundredth birthday
in *Jalna,* she could hardly be kept alive much longer. After a
family quarrel over Grandmother's giving a family ring to
Pheasant, old Mrs. Whiteoak and Mr. Fennel, the minister, settled down to a game of backgammon. Though he won the game,
she refused to admit defeat, even maintained she had won.
The omniscient observer related how the old woman was looking
at Finch. "Her eyes were saying to him: 'A Court afraid? A
Court afraid of death? Gammon!' " In an eccentric domestic
touch, her parrot shook himself and a feather "fluttered to the
floor" (228). The Grandmother's head sank, and she was dead.

Miss de la Roche demonstrated in the death scene and in the
Grandmother, a deft Dickensian touch. In the tradition of the
great Victorian novelist, she presented a forceful character,
slightly caricatured, who powerfully grasped the readers' imagination.

III   Finch's Fortune

Miss de la Roche could march along, chronologically, with her

Whiteoaks, for a time. Her next installment, *Finch's Fortune*, in 1931, posed essentially the same question which always began "Our Gal Sunday": "Can an artistic young man from Ontario find happiness after inheriting his grandmother's fortune?" The advertising writer for Pan Books stated the themes baldly enough for the most simple-minded schoolgirl to understand: "At twenty-one Finch Whiteoak, proud, sensitive, reckless, becomes the bewildered inheritor of his grandmother's fortune. In this enthralling episode from the Whiteoaks saga, the ever generous Finch takes his two Uncles to England, and against a lovely Devonshire background, falls in and out of love with the bewitching Sarah Court, suffering all the youthful agonies of disillusion and frustrated passion." The Pan cover was magnificently conceived: Finch and Sarah were standing on the wind-swept heath, with billowing clouds overhead. His face was not to be seen, for he was embracing her; but she had a look of ecstasy on her face.

Though Finch was attracted to his cousin Sarah, she married Arthur Leigh. Finch accompanied them on their honeymoon. Arthur had insisted on the *menage à trois* in these words: "I want the woman I love and the man I love beside me. I want the two different loves merged into one beautiful whole" (163). During this speech, Arthur held Finch's hand tightly. Miss de la Roche's ardent fans were apparently stout-hearted enough to read such discrete intimations of homosexuality.

On the honeymoon, the three were caught in a squall and saw lovers in a hedge. To Finch, "The man's head had been still as the upraised head of a snake about to sting" (173). When Arthur went to get the car, Finch and Sarah declared their love for each other; the waves were thundering on the beach below. Finch, however, was not to transform himself into a viper; instead, he declared that Arthur was his best friend and was not to know of his love for Sarah.

Back at Jalna, Alayne, who had divorced Eden and married Renny, was having great difficulties in adjusting to her new life. She left him to return to New York, but could not stay away from her man. Renny's affections were wandering, and a Clara Lebraux had taken his eye. Meanwhile the Wall Street Crash of 1929 was having its effects in Canada, and the Whiteoaks were hard pressed for cash. When Finch returned, the family learned he had spent on relatives or lost on investments and loans most of the fourtune left him by his grandmother. Though beset by financial problems, family life continued. The second son of Piers and Pheasant was healthy and named Finch. The Whiteoak clan was destined to go on. Artistically, Miss de la Roche had come to a most advantageous place to end her Jalna saga. But with the urging of publishers and readers, she chose not to do so.

IV *The Series*

Miss de la Roche began to realize that if she wanted to go on making her living off the Whiteoaks, she needed to deal with them not only in the near present but also in the past; that is, before the beginning of the first volume of the series. If one wanted to read the Jalna books in the chronological order of the Whiteoak family tree, he should proceed thusly:

(1) *The Building of Jalna*
(2) *Morning at Jalna*
(3) *Mary Wakefield*
(4) *Young Renny*
(5) *Whiteoak Heritage*
(6) *The Whiteoak Brothers*
(7) *Jalna*
(8) *Whiteoaks of Jalna*
(9) *Finch's Fortune*
(10) *The Master of Jalna*
(11) *Whiteoak Harvest*
(12) *Wakefield's Course*
(13) *Return to Jalna*
(14) *Renny's Daughter*
(15) *Variable Winds at Jalna*
(16) *Centenary at Jalna.*

If, however, the reader wanted to read the novels in the order in which they were written, he should arrange them in this order:

(1) *Jalna* (1927)
(2) *Whiteoaks of Jalna* (1929)
(3) *Finch's Fortune* (1931)

While most of the volumes, after the first three in the series, are certainly less fresh, they contain scattered incidents which are of some interest: there are scenes of comic relief and occasional good dramatic episodes; there is an embarrassing imitation of *Jane Eyre;* there is shameless exploitation of the American Civil War and a glossing over of the 1930's; there is a total immersion in Playland; and there are touches of incest and sadism. There is no real indication, however, that Miss de la Roche's narrative style or artistic understanding were much different in 1960 than in 1927. If her literary abilities progressed at all, the direction was downward. The remaining thirteen novels of the Jalna series are discussed, therefore, in the order of the Whiteoak family chronology.

V   The Building of Jalna

Devoted fans would clearly have an interest in the building of the Whiteoak family home and in knowing more about Philip and Adeline in their prime. In 1944, Miss de la Roche invited her readers to partake of that part of the romance. With a great deal of material to present, the author devoted the early part of *The Building of Jalna* to explaining about the background of Adeline and Philip, their meeting in India, their marriage, and their decision to emigrate to Canada; and there was virtually no attempt to dramatize any of this material. In the section set in Ireland, however, where the young couple went to visit her parents, the readers met Lady Honora, Adeline's mother, and Renny, Adeline's quick-tempered father; and the action became dramatic, not narrative. A tremendous amount of space was then devoted to the trip to Canada, to storms at sea, to the death of the baby's nurse, to the elopement of Adeline's brother. As usual, Miss de la Roche filled her novel with characters who do not really advance the action of the story; rigorous artistic discipline is completely missing.

The novel, in fact, lopes along in the usual episodic form. The Whiteoaks, who had made their first home in Quebec, suddenly decided to find a milder climate and moved to Ontario. The Quebec scenes add nothing but words to the novel. At their newly purchased estate, the grand house Jalna arose while the Whiteoaks lived with their friends the Vaughans. David Vaughan wanted to attract congenial people to the area and "establish the customs and traditions of England, to be enjoyed and cherished by their descendants." (92) To these customs he would somehow add the freedom of the New Land.

As the readers had every right to expect, Daisy, a young relative of the Vaughans, flirted with Philip. Adeline had a platonic affair with James Wilmott, who had been on board ship with them and had bought a cabin nearby. Wilmott himself is not particularly interesting—he had deserted his shrewish wife and disgusting daughter to begin life anew in Canada. His servant, an Indian half-breed named Titus Sharrow, however, is a comic character of interest. Miss de la Roche rather belabors his beauty, and he is clearly the same kind of virile, Lawrencian gamekeeper-type she used earlier in *Possession*. He is presented as liar and thief—stock characteristics for a half-breed—but as one who lies charmingly, amusing those he wrongs. After Daisy had literally thrown herself upon Philip at a picnic, Adeline invited Daisy to go riding with her and severely thrashed the girl. Daisy disappeared for a few days. The reader learns she was hidden away with Titus, but Miss de la Roche showed great restraint and did not describe the rutting in the forest. Titus was able to tell a half-way convincing lie about finding Daisy, and the reader must provide her own gamekeeper-lady scenes.

In this novel, the comic incidents (and the scenes are intentionally comic) are of more interest than the romantic stories about the founding of the dynasty. Mrs. Wilmott traced her husband to Ontario. The snobbish Mrs. Wilmott's lines run like these: "My father, Mr. Peter Quinton, he is descended from Sir Ralph Quinton who was a great inventor and scientist of the sixteenth century—you may have heard of him—I mean Sir Ralph, of course, not my father. Not that I should say my father is not a man of some importance, for he has stood for his borough more than once and been not too badly defeated" (139-140). In the presence of such a fool, Adeline had no hesitation in lying. James Wilmott, she reported, had lived nearby in a log cabin; but he had gone to Mexico and there died. Mrs. Wilmott left to continue the search but finally devoted all her energies to the Abolitionist movement in the United States.

James Wilmott remained a devoted admirer of Adeline, but his love was never expressed in physical terms. Instead, he was cared for by the charming half-breed, Titus. Again Miss de la Roche returned to that happy state in which people of the same sex lived contentedly together. "It is enough for me, Boss, . . . Just to live here alone with you . . .," Titus said after he returned from his idyll with Daisy. Wilmott declared, "I'm very fond of you," and Titus responded, "And I am very fond of you, also, Boss. Like mine, your eyelashes are long and your neck like a bronze column." Miss de la Roche groped invariably for the phallic image.

The house did get built, and Adeline had her third baby there; the church was constructed; Lord Elgin came for a visit. The building of the estate and the founding of the Whiteoak dynasty are in the best romantic tradition, but the comic scenes (intrinsically more interesting) are not really integrated into the novel.

Reviews for the novel were extremely favorable. A typical one was by Sterling North in *Book Week,* October 29, 1944; "One . . . has the uncanny feeling that in another incarnation he has lived in Jalna, has sipped hot tea and eaten buttered scones, helped with foaling mares, shared the moments of rage and tenderness of the cantankerous and lovable brood. It is a great saga." (2).

VI   Morning at Jalna

Morning at Jalna (1960) is perhaps Miss de la Roche's greatest failure in the series. It is as if her editors had told her, "Civil War Novels Sell." But how to get *Gone-With-The-Wind*-like characters and the romantic war to Canada? Farfetched, indeed, but Miss de la Roche's imagination found a way: the Whiteoaks had met the Sinclairs in England, where both families were visiting, and had invited the Sinclairs for a visit. In 1863, their Carolinian friends (it is not certain whether North or South) came for a visit, bringing with them three of their slaves. Mr. Sinclair was not quite the Rhett or even the Ashley type, for he was a hunchback (for no particular reason, it seems, except to keep him out of the Confederate Army). However, he did have his attractions, as this discussion with its phallic implications shows: He laid his hand on his wife's knee. "Always had she admired the thumb in particular. It was almost as long as a finger and perfectly rounded, the nail showing a half moon" (11).

As one might expect, the Whiteoaks sympathized with the Southern cause and believed the Negroes liked being slaves. (Miss de la Roche, as writer, did nothing to indicate that slavery was despicable.) To add drama to the visit of the plantation owners and their slaves, Miss de la Roche revealed that Mr. Sinclair was an agent of Jefferson Davis and had been sent to organize raids against Yankee shipping in the Great Lakes! On Mr. Sinclair's first excursion (after some mysterious comings and goings of Confederate agents at Jalna), he was captured off estate, as it were. Miss de la Roche just did not know enough about the United States in the nineteenth century or of the Civil War to describe his capture and detention by the Yankees, who, the reader is constantly told in the novel, lacked manners.

As a Civil War epic, the novel was a fiasco; but one sub-plot was well done. Titus was again introduced as a comic half-breed. He reminded Wilmott that Daisy had told him his mouth was "like a pomegranate flower." Wilmott didn't want to be reminded of that affair, and Tite (as he was called) replied, "That was years ago, and I am of a more noble character now. You have heard of the noble red man, boss?" (43). Titus was attracted to the slave Annabelle, but was warned by Wilmott to stay away from her. But Titus, intent upon seducing the attractive mulatto (her grandfather was white), became religious to further his aims. Titus found unexpected difficulties though. He took Annabelle boating, declared he loved both God and her. After he found a bank covered with flowers, they sank to the grass. She felt confident of her handsome suitor, proud that her hair was not wooly, and she looked admiringly at "his rounded brown neck." As he whispered for her not to be afraid, his "hand pressed her ribs." And the Whiteoaks children came crashing into the love nest wanting to know if Tite and Annabelle were having a picnic. "Not yet," Tite said (67).

Miss de la Roche succeeded admirably in turning the seduction scene into farce. When she allowed the two to marry, she drew back from describing their love-making. Instead she had Annabelle spend her time in bed crying because of her real or imagined sins. Titus took her to the reservation and sold her to a cousin, a religious man; she was, Titus explained, accustomed to being bought and sold. Wilmott, though upset at first, was in fact relieved; for he had been jealous of Annabelle's part in Titus' life. The two men were together again; the slim moon shone silver light on them, and Titus said, "It seems to me, boss, that you and I are not marrying men. We are so happy in the company of each other. A woman is quite *de trop*" (259).

But the theme of manly love and the comic character of Titus do not fit the Civil War theme. Nor does the long scene describing the honeymoon of Mr. Madigan, tutor of the children, and Amelia Busby, daughter of a local Abolitionist. On their wedding trip, "intoxicated by abstinence from drink and indulgence in animal gratification" (86), Madigan revealed Mr. Sinclair's plans to raid Northern shipping. The reasons for his giving away the secret are, one suspects, unintentionally comic; but, at any rate, Amelia clung to her husband until he was asleep, then stole away to tell the Yankees of Mr. Sinclair's plan.

After Mr. Sinclair's capture, it was feared he would be executed; but he was sent home and Mrs. Sinclair left Jalna to join him. Their plantations were in ruin; but when at the end of the novel, just after the war had ended, the Whiteoaks sailed for Europe, the Sinclair's were on board and prosperous. And why were they rich? "Sinclair's father sent cotton to Manchester," Philip explained (268). Nonsense, readers are to think, the South was not impoverished. Reconstruction did not happen. The Southern aristocrats did not lose their money.

Kirkus reported of *Morning at Jalna,* on July 1, 1960, "However cliché the meandering plot, it is a skillful and harmless story-telling for that abiding audience" (529). One assumes the "abiding audience" was unconcerned about the howling historical blunders. *The Times Literary Supplement*, July 29, 1960, said more tartly that one would not be squeamish about the novel—"unless one cares about literature." The reviewer finally concluded, however, "The Jalna marathon has, indeed, moved outside the range of literary criteria" (447).

VII   Mary Wakefield

As her invention began to flag, after she had rung the changes of Finch and Whiteoak and Piers, of Pheasant and Renny, and of all the other Whiteoaks in book after book, Miss de la Roche turned to an imitation of one of the great Victorian classics she had read as a child. In *Mary Wakefield* (1949) she used archetypal scenes from *Jane Eyre*: a plain governess came to a strange household; she found there a fascinating Master, impediments to marriage, a second suitor, and, finally, happiness with the Master.

Unlike Jane Eyre, Mary was not given a credible background. And, instead of Miss Brontë's brilliant social criticism as she dissected Lowood School and the real but Gothic horrors of nineteenth-century England, Miss de la Roche gave the reader a comfortable feeling about poverty. The death of Mary's father left her without funds, but the horrors which should have befallen her did not. She became a governess to the Whiteoak children, Renny and Meg, and went to Canada. Miss de la Roche could not devise a fine Byronic hero even remotely similar to Rochester of *Jane Eyre* for the Whiteoak family tree made it imperative that Mary fall in love with weak, pouting Philip, who was more akin to Lord Ingram than Rochester.

Instead of the mad wife of *Jane Eyre* as an impediment to marriage, Miss de la Roche used Adeline Court Whiteoak; and, instead of the famous scene in which the Jane-Rochester marriage was stopped, Miss de la Roche had Adeline walk out of the church when the Banns were read. In anger, Mary told Mrs. Whiteoak that she was Philip's mistress. Miss Brontë's scene was more dramatic and more significant: Rochester wanted Jane to live with him without benefit of clergy. Mary's second suitor could not be called a cardboard figure—he was as flimsy as tissue paper; needed for love interest, he was trotted into the novel; no longer needed, he disappeared. St. John Rivers of *Jane Eyre* for all of his eccentricity and in spite of the unbelievable coincidence of Jane's coming to his house, was believable, in comparison to Miss de la Roche's second suitor.

It would appear that powerful scenes from *Jane Eyre* stuck in Miss de la Roche's mind; when she needed key scenes, she used those of the novel in her own fashion but with weakened effectiveness. Mary ran away from Jalna, but she did not encounter the horrors of Jane's flight; she merely got somewhat hot and dusty. Miss de la Roche seems to have learned nothing of the artistic method from *Jane Eyre;* she could not create the banter of Rochester and Jane. Instead of the high Gothic horror of the mad wife trying to set Rochester afire, Miss de la Roche wrote, because it fitted into the scheme of her Whiteoak saga, the domestic drama. Mary is a pale imitation (and imitation she definitely is) of Jane, but the imitation is without artistic merit of any kind. Miss de la Roche's novel will certainly never be discussed for its literary merits. (Miss de la Roche dramatized the novel under the title *The Mistress of Jalna*. It was produced in England and Canada [2] but was not a success.) There are, unfortunately, no comic characters equal to Titus to relieve the melodrama of the story.

VIII   Young Renny

Another way to keep the series going was to enliven the scene with the outrageous. In *Young Renny (Jalna—*1906) (1935) Miss de la Roche introduced a semi-villain: Cousin Malahide, an eccentric Irishman who resembled Ichabod Crane. His sex was indeterminate: did he wear corsets to keep a slim waist? He was fond of malicious gossip, not unlike a vicious woman.

In this episode of the saga, Miss de la Roche dramatized Meg's refusal to marry Maurice because he had fathered an illegitimate child. Before the child was born, Renny, acting as Maurice's emissary, tried to pay the girl off and became fascinated with her aunt/sister/mother (the relationship is not clear) who was fathered by a Hungarian gypsy! Lulu, the gypsy, later seduced Renny; and the boy was found out, largely because of Cousin Malahide. The non-virgin Renny had to face family and friends, who were horrified: A common woman and in a hay loft!

The most successful serious scene—the finding of the illegitimate child on the Vaughan's doorstep, the seduction of Renny by the gaudy gypsy, the dramatic horse race between Renny and Cousin Malahide were all set pieces—occurred when Adeline and her son Philip aired the clothes of the long-dead Captain Philip Whiteoak. The episode is Dickensian in its intensity. As the clothes were unpacked and brushed, son Philip found that the coat his father wore the day he died was filled with moth holes and needed to be destroyed. Adeline was deeply moved by the memories of the clothes, and young Philip said he would burn the coat in the woods, where his father hunted. As he took the coat away, Miss de la Roche probed his thoughts: "What was death? Was it his father's hand reaching out through the sleeve of the coat to grasp his and draw him into that blackness where he would be effaced? Or was it his father living on in him, striding as he strode, over the land they loved?" (207). This scene is amazingly well done; and as counterpoint, Miss de la Roche has Renny shoot the old mare, the suffering animal he had been told to destroy days before, but in his youth had tried to save, though he had only prolonged the misery of the beast. As has been noted, Miss de la Roche had undeniable talent for heightening scenes and playing the dramatic elements in them. In many instances, the effect is unintentionally ludicrous, but the sentiment is quite believable in the incident of the coat.

As she often did, Miss de la Roche also inserted comic scenes. The best of these have to do with the pranks of Renny and Meg on tattling Malahide. They secretly enraged a swan, which then attacked Malahide. When the swan gave chase, Malahide lost his balance and fell into the stream: "In a second the swan was on top of him, and such a confusion of beating wings, contorted neck, and threshing legs and arms ensued that, for a space, nothing could be distinguished through the sheet of upthrown water . . . Gathering all his force, Malahide was able to free himself for a moment and scrambled frantically to the shore. The swan . . .rocked ferociously in his wake. Malahide leaped to gain the trunk of a tree, but the swan, with a grand spread of his wings, leaped too and bore him to earth" (287).

[76]

The humor of the novel was again in the frontier tradition Miss de la Roche had used in *Delight*.

Her American publishers, not happy with the novel, were reluctant to publish it; she revised it slightly, omitting a lisp here, eccentricities there. Mr. Hambleton quotes a letter of Miss de la Roche noting that Daniel Macmillan "thought it equal to the others in the series" (157) and had the book published. Mr. Macmillan was correct: it was equal to the others in the series. Only its Dickensian qualities and the scenes of frontier comedy are praiseworthy.

Not all the reviewers were happy that Miss de la Roche had broken the Whiteoak chronology for the first time. James Hanley in *Time and Tide* for May 11, 1935, wrote: "It came as something of a shock to me to find old Adeline, the eighty year old grandmother . . . grinning with senile archness from its pages, after having last read of her as dead and decently buried. . ." He also noted that food was the panacea for all the ills of the Whiteoak family; when Meg was hysterical because of Maurice Vaughan's bastard child, the family tried to soothe her by leaving trays filled with tempting foods outside her door. With irony he observed, "Presumably the trays win in the end, for Meg re-appears and life continues with its habitual gusto."

IX   Whiteoak Heritage

Whiteoak Heritage (1940) is an almost perfect example of a novel illustrating the adolescent image of love in all its most passionate forms. *Young Renny* was set in 1906; *Whiteoak Heritage* was set immediately after World War I. The story began with Renny and Maurice Vaughan returning from the war; Renny, to a mismanaged estate, for his father and stepmother had died, leaving Jalna to the care of the uncles and the ancient grandmother; Maurice, to his illegitimate daughter. Two main love stories were introduced: Renny's half-brother Eden, now a university student, was infatuated with Mrs. Stroud, an Older-Woman-Sexually-Frustrated-Because-Her-Late-Husband-Had-Long-Been-An-Invalid; Renny had become enamoured of Christine, supposedly the sister but in actuality the wife of Jim, one of Renny's employees in the stable. Christine and Jim lived in half of Mrs. Stroud's house. Miss de la Roche here introduced the image of the divided house which she used later in *A Boy in the House*. She used tangled sexual relationships in both: in *A Boy in the House*, the writer who rented part of the house from two old ladies was madly infatuated with the Home Boy living with them; in *Whiteoak Heritage*, Jim and Christine pretended to be brother and sister because he received one hundred pounds a year from a wealthy Englishwoman if he remained unmarried. The walls were thin, however; and Mrs. Stroud, who learned the truth, told all to the Other Woman in England.

The love scenes between Christine and Renny were girlishly romantic. When Christine took a nighttime, nude swim in Lake Ontario, the waves "were a dozen wild horses careening about her, never to be broken in. She gave herself up to her joy in them"(126). When she lost her footing, Renny appeared to rescue her, and the waves beat against them; then came "a lull in the agitation of the waves that, in contrast to the former sonorous roar, was almost silence." (127) The sexual scene was thus described before the act itself took place. In fact, there was no reason for any other description. Renny walked up the beach, threw himself down on his stomach (Miss de la Roche has forgotten to tell us whether or not he had in the meantime shucked off his clothes) and Christine came to him. "He turned over on his back and smiled up at her. He put both arms about her" (128). In the next sentence, it was after midnight and Renny was seeing Christine home. Readers of all ages are left to speculate on Renny as stallion. James Jones, a generation later, in that romantic novel *From Here to Eternity* wrote a similar, though slightly more explicit, love scene set on a beach.

Repressed Mrs. Stroud was not so fortunate as Christine; she was unable to get Eden to bed, though his artistic nature had not made him neuter. The Whiteoaks, hoping to destroy the unseemly affair, sent Uncle Ernest to court her. He could give her intellectual companionship, could talk of Shakespeare (she was *mad* about literature), but could not (he was old) or would not (he was a confirmed bachelor) relieve her sexual frustrations. In the only mildly comic scene in the novel, the two suitors—Eden and Ernest—tried to outstay each other at Mrs. Stroud's until the tension finally made her send them home.

When they returned to Jalna, they duelled for her; mock-heroically, they rolled dice for her. Eden won.

When Eden was finally found out (he claimed his prize by taking her almost daily on canoe rides in the lake), he was forbidden by Renny to see Mrs. Stroud again. Mrs. Stroud then imagined that Renny might be the one for her. In the stables at Jalna, however, she saw her Intended kissing Christine. In her fury, she turned the horse, Launceton, being trained for the Grand National, out into the snow to die.

But evil in Jalnaland was not quite evil. Mrs. Stroud was driven away. Eden was out of his entanglement. Gran Whiteoak decided to pay the passage of Christine and Jim Dayborn back to England, where, it was hoped, the patroness could be placated. Renny was thus saved from a prolonged affair with a married woman. All was well at Jalna again.

A review in the Macmillan Clipping Books in London demonstrates why the religious took comfort in the novels. The *Church Times* in 1940 praised the novel because family life was upheld "in a period considered notorious for the decline of real family life. . ." The irony of such a statement is delightful.

X   The Whiteoak Brothers

The Whiteoak Brothers (Jalna 1923) (1953) centered on budding young poet Eden. As was usual with Miss de la Roche when dealing with artists, she told the reader that Eden was a poet of promise; but she did not explore the creative process. He wanted to escape the stifling influences of family and university and was innocently used by a mining broker to sell shares of Indigo Lake Mine. The Pan "blurb" writer once again caught the right note for the cover: "One by one Eden persuades the Whiteoaks to part with their savings, even old Adeline. Each is anxious to conceal it from the others . . . and Jalna becomes electric with secrecy and excited expectation." When Mr. Kronk, the broker, abscounded, the Whiteoaks suffered great financial loss. Renny, however, had not known of the scheme. There is little feeling for the speculative 1920's in the novel; speculation and human greed are merely made melodramatic, and social reality is not to be found. Indeed, even the two romances interwoven in the novel are tame. Piers' growing love for Maurice Vaughan's illegitimate daughter, Pheasant, and Dilly Warkworth's infatuation with Renny, who was not interested in her.

The Macmillan Clipping File in London contains about forty reviews of the novel, mostly from provincial newspapers; and almost all the reviews spoke of the great pleasure of reading about the "well-loved" Whiteoaks again. Prosaic as the novel was, it is clear that Miss de la Roche's devoted fans were willing and eager to read any fragment of Jalna history. In the United States, *Time,* November 30, 1953, explained her popularity thusly: "Author de la Roche's achievement seems to be that she knows that Jalna's changeless orchards, spaniels, horses and horseplay are just what a lot of city-pent readers are grateful for." The reviewer decided, however, that the novels were "beyond artistic criticism" (104).

NOTE: In the family chronology of the Whiteoaks, *Jalna, Whiteoaks of Jalna,* and *Finch's Fortune* belong here.

XI   The Master of Jalna

The Master of Jalna, (1933) was written during the early depression years of the 1930's, and the time supposedly was the present. Times were presumably hard, but one could scarcely tell it from the way the Whiteoaks lived. True, they had a little difficulty paying their bills, Alayne's stocks no longer paid dividends, and the market value of their farm crops was depressed. But they continued to have servants (though their salaries were in arrears), and their bountiful meals and teas were not diminished.

In truth, the story is set in the timeless world of the imagination; and it is clear that Miss de la Roche, who was at the peak of her popularity in the 1930's, did not really understand the misery, degradation, and suffering that gripped much of the Western world. The millions of unemployed and the breadlines did not find even the faintest reflection in this novel. Instead, the plot had to do with the deaths of Eden and Aunt Augusta, Renny's tangled relations with Clara Lebraux and her daughter, Finch's attraction and repulsion for Sarah, and the effects of Maurice Vaughan's plans for a housing development near Jalna. Though in skeletal outline the plot seems rather extreme for one novel, it is less confused and tangled than some of the others in the series.

Arthur Leigh was killed off conveniently in a boating accident, leaving his enigmatic widow Sarah with great amounts of money. Naturally, her stocks had not declined. The Whiteoaks talked endlessly about which brother should go forth as a suitor—Eden had returned to Vaughanlands (he can not be in Piers' presence because of the Eden-Pheasant affair) from his wanderings in Europe, and Finch was about to burst into the world as a great pianist. Finch was thrown together with Sarah most often, but he was at first more than reluctant. Her late husband had been his ardent suitor, then his rival who stole her away. Finch was shown to be as uncertain, unstable, and neurotic, as all great artists are reputed to be.

Eden, also in the fashion of poets, was again suffering from tuberculosis, and died in his bedroom, after hemorrhaging and other such sufferings, with Renny as messenger to tell the audience. The funeral was described in detail; and, to show the family wounds finally healed, Piers was one of the pall bearers. Aunt Augusta who also died away from the prying eyes of the readers, fortunately left a sizeable fortune to Uncle Ernest and Nicholas. With twelve hundred pounds a year now added to the family fortunes, could one really believe in the Great Depression? Wouldn't it be nice to think that every semi-impoverished, every starving family in 1933 would suddenly inherit money from a titled relative.

Another part of the story had to do with Clara Lebraux and her daughter Pauline. Wakefield was in love with the daughter, but she was in love with Renny. The neighborhood was beginning to gossip about Renny and Clara, but nothing really happened between those two until after a great crisis at Jalna. Maurice Vaughan was having financial difficulties and decided to subdivide his estate. Two houses were actually under construction, but the buildings were pictured as inferior; and the elder Whiteoaks, at least, insisted that the new tenants would spoil the neighborhood. When Alayne would not lend money to buy the property, Renny took the money from Sarah, giving her a mortgage on Jalna. When he also proposed to move Mrs. Lebraux and the foxes she grew to the new property, Alayne was less than gracious. His family and his wife angry at him, he naturally had a brief affair with Clara: " 'This will be our bed,' he said, indicating the pine-needles" (251).

Betwixt the more flamboyant happenings in the story, Miss de la Roche filled in with accounts of Renny's young daughter Adeline, a trial to her mother, but a true descendant of the old grandmother. Clearly, the author wanted the readers to antici- pate the day when the small girl would be as commanding a figure as her spirited ancestor.

Allan Nevins in the *Saturday Review of Literature*, Septem- ber 16, 1933, was in agreement with most of the other review- ers when he praised the "dexterously drawn" and "self-willed characters" presented by Miss de la Roche. He admired the vig- or with which she presented "the power of kinship, family pride, and the sense of a common past. . ." (109).

XII   Whiteoak Harvest

Whiteoak Harvest (1936) is an absolute return to Playland. Alayne found Renny in what she wrongly interpreted as a compromising situation with Clara Lebraux. He admitted that Clara had been his lover some months before but was no long- er. Alayne would not be pacified. Wakefield, now a handsome young man, had planned to marry Clara's daughter, Pauline, who was secretly in love with Renny. Wakefield had become a Catholic convert; and, though he was in no way shown to be in- trospective or torn by religious doubts, he decided he could not marry but must enter a monastery; Pauline decided to enter a nunnery.

Adding to these soap opera details was the formless subplot concerning Finch, now a famous pianist, and his bride Sarah, who came to Jalna and took up part of the action, while Alayne fled her husband to live with an aunt in New York. Finch and Sarah brought with them Roma, Eden's illegitimate child, who was previously unknown to the family. She became playmate for Adeline, daughter of Renny and Alayne, a child as imper- ious as her grandmother was. What was most curious about Finch was his growing inability to be near Sarah; he would no longer sleep with her and retreated to the confines of his child- hood bedroom. He could no longer bear to hear her play the vio- lin. Sarah insisted that Renny was the cause of the estrangement; he was deliberately keeping them apart. To add more drama to this melodrama, Sarah held the mortgage on Jalna.

Sarah sent Finch a consulting specialist. Miss de la Roche knew exactly what her readers in the 1930's wanted to read about psychiatrists: "He was a spare, grey-faced man who looked rather ill himself. He had neither heart, humour, nor understanding, and did well in the diagnosis of sensitive patients" (145). He prescribed ultra-violet ray treatment and apparently the readers were to feel that the penetrating light would reveal the secret devils raging in Finch, giving him his headaches, keeping him in his room away from wife and family.

The plot moved rapidly. Clara sold her things and went away. She advised Renny to forget his pride, go to New York, and request that Alayne return to Jalna. He followed her suggestion; but, when he arrived, he found Alayne almost eight months pregnant. In this sudsy opera, the child was his. A current television soap opera, however, would discuss other possible sires for several episodes. Renny returned to Jalna with Alayne and her aunt, Miss Archer, whose money had just disappeared in the depression.

Once home at Jalna, all was well again. Finch, who was now recovering from his breakdown, gave Renny the last of his inheritance to pay off the mortgage and became well again. Finch thought: "What has broken the chains that held me to fear and pain? I don't need to ask myself this. It is because I have given away the last of Gran's money . . . I've been so morbidly wrapped up in my own suffering that I have forgotten the suffering of others" (245). Such sentiments were undoubtedly consoling to readers during the depression of 1936. In a melodramatic scene, Renny took the money to Sarah in cash, and she tried to throw it in the fire. But, though it is comforting for the poor to believe money brings pain, it is not proper to destroy it; Renny saved the bills and locked them in a drawer.

The last chapter of the novel was the most romantically conceived in the Jalna series. At a dinner party given before Wakefield was to take his final vows, Uncle Ernest announced he had proposed to Miss Archer and had been accepted. Wakefield had an announcement also; he rose dramatically, unbuttoned his novice's robe, and stood before his family wearing dinner clothes. He was not to take his final orders after all. The scene is just the sort of adolescent dream presented seriously in countless novels and movies. But Miss de la Roche could hardly be faulted for desiring such a dramatic conclusion since such an ending kept her from alienating her English-oriented readers! Wakefield remained a Catholic—bad enough for Anglo-Saxons—but he was not leaving the world. And, after all, he did have long eyelashes and dramatic talent and belonged in Hollywood. To keep everyone comfortable in these dark days of the world depression, Renny stayed in the dining room briefly, kissed the picture of his grandmother, and said: "It's all right, old lady. Everything's going fine" (255).

XII   Wakefield's Course

Wakefield's Course (1941) is held together loosely by the buying of the horse that will win the Grand National for the Whiteoaks. The novel is *National Velvet,* without a young, slim Elizabeth Taylor. Instead of Miss Taylor and England in glorious technicolor, the reader has Ireland, Canada, and England in highly colored descriptions. The most promising part of the story has to do with the visit of Wakefield (now a London actor) and Finch (preparing for a great concert) to Cousin Malahide's crumbling Irish estate. Lisping, mincing, Cousin Malahide is somehow even more evil than he had appeared in *Young Renny,* but this promise of Jamesian, Gothic evil is not fulfilled. Malahide was to get a commission on a horse being offered to Renny and was on good behaviour one supposes.

Unkown to Finch, another guest at Malahide's damp pile was his own wife Sarah, and the first night in Ireland, she appeared to him, coming through a cupboard. After such a Gothic entrance, he could hardly do anything except cast aside all his revulsion for her, and they were soon abed. But not before Wakefield had peered into the room and seen Finch kneeling; he had thought him praying when in fact Finch was kissing his long-hated, now loved wife! (65)

The action was rather slow in this novel, much given to nature description in Ireland and Wales and to the theatrical world in London. Wakefield auditioned for a part in a play, received it, and played opposite a young lady who much attracted him.

[84]

When Renny arrived in London after buying the horse, he kept looking at the girl, thereby arousing Wakefield's jealousy. But the plot meandered along. Finch and Sarah were now happy, but Wakefield and Renny distrusted Sarah. Wakefield's play was a success, as was Finch's concert. There were a few hints of war in the dialogue, but Miss de la Roche was no more successful in suggesting that period just before World War II than she was with the Great Depression. (In fact, the continuing financial troubles of the late 1930's were completely missing in this story. Jalna folk were affluent again, ready to pay vast sums for horses and trips abroad.) Miss de la Roche moved along slowly, waiting to introduce her grand theme of the novel.

Sex, as has already been noted, was common in each novel, most often the explicit scenes being heterosexual passions; but in this novel, Miss de la Roche worked up to a typical nineteenth-century horror theme: incest. Wakefield, one discovers, was in love with Molly, Renny's illegitimate daughter by Christine, the horse trainer in *Whiteoak Heritage*. Therefore, the two could not marry. Everyone at Jalna learned, for the first time, of Renny's indiscretion. The Pan blurb writer, always eager to grab the attention of a prospective purchaser, wrote; "Two star-crossed lovers face an agonizing decision in this surging episode in the history of one of fiction's best-loved families. . ." Later, as will be seen, Wakefield and Molly do live together, without benefit of clergy. A few of Miss de la Roche's adoring fans objected to the incestuous relationship but most of her readers undoubtedly regarded it as in the romantic tradition of Lord Byron's affair with his half-sister.

The war did begin; and Renny, Piers, and Wakefield all went off to it. Renny's horse won the Grand National. Renny was a war hero. Wakefield, also a war hero, was decorated by the King. Piers, another war hero, was captured by the Germans. There will always be an England.

Despite the trite action and the sexual irregularities of the novel, the *Christian Science Monitor* for October 18, 1941, praised its domestic and religious scenes (10). Mary Ross in *Books*, September 28, 1941, declared she was "as avid for further news of the Whiteoaks as for news of actual friends" (3).

XIV   Return to Jalna

In *Return to Jalna*, (1946), all the men-who-went-marching-off-to-World-War-II came home again, and before the war's end. They were, of course, heroes all; but their fate was to be the fate of the soap-opera heroes. Wakefield, after years of flying, had a heart attack and needed rest. Piers, who had lost a leg to the Germans, worried that he had been unmanned but proved himself by siring another child. Renny had a concussion and suffered from lapses of memory, a favorite ploy of soap-opera writers; and Miss de la Roche was not one to avoid such a fine device. Traditionalist Renny fought modern encroachments on the secluded Jalna estate. Meg (recently widowed) sold Vaughanlands to Mr. Clapperton, a despicable businessman, who decided to subdivide the property and erect a model town. Renny feared his whole idyllic world would end: "Renny would perch on the boundary fence and watch the tiny settlement with malevolent interest. . . .The baby in the nearest house was screaming louder. The radio in the next little house never stopped grinding out raucous music. He pictured how, as the city grew, more and more people would be inclined to come here, till at last there would be no privacy and no peace." (193-94).

After Renny had a particularly heated verbal altercation with Mr. Clapperton, the businessman discovered one thousand dollars missing, and a twenty dollar bill fell out of Renny's pocket at the time he denied the accusation. Bills began appearing here and there. Had Renny stolen during one of his lapses of memory? A Queen of the Soap Opera writers could have extended the psychoanalysis for weeks. Miss de la Roche was up to the challenge, and her characters talked the subject dry at the dinner table, tea table, in private conversations in bedrooms, and in local gossip. But the solution to the theft came when Mr. Fennel, pastor of the church, had Renny in for a bit of prayer; Renny on the same day discovered that Roma, the illegitimate daughter of Eden, had stolen the money to help her Uncle! Miss de la Roche undoubtedly knew that her readers wanted to believe in the efficacy of prayer.

Renny managed to save Jalna and the Whiteoak Way of Life by persuading Clapperton's fiancée that the model village would eventually be a slum; she made her future husband promise not to continue the project. Renny was unsympathetic with the need for housing after World War II. What did he care? He had saved his estate. It is clear that Miss de la Roche, in her presentation of this material, was using Renny as her spokesman. Time after time, in these later novels, Miss de la Roche was holding up to scorn the present world. Biscuits had lost their taste, music was depraved, Americans were barbarians. Her news could comfort the middle aged who read her novels.

A scene from her own autobiography became a central incident in this novel: Mama and Papa de la Roche read *Othello* until the lines became too risque, they thought, for their young daughter. In the novel, Adeline, the beautiful young daughter, was taken by her cousin Maurice, now the heir to an Irish fortune, and by his tutor, Mr. Clapperton's obnoxious secretary, to see Paul Robeson in *Othello*

Adeline was excited by the story, but not by the gamy lines; and Sidney, the secretary, excited by the sexuality of the play, attempted to make love to Adeline. She struggled, and Papa Renny appeared to give the young man a good thrashing. Although Miss de la Roche constantly dramatized and adapted scenes from her life as she wrote the family chronicle, she heightened them considerably in recasting the incidents.

The story wandered along in a friendly fashion, evoking tears here and there as the brothers Whiteoak returned home from the wars. Only the most devoted readers could have had much incentive to see how each Whiteoak male, wife, and kin would adapt to the world after the war. Indeed, a few of the critics had begun to tire; A. E. Gasaway in *Bookweek* for October 27, 1946, noted, "Although the Jalna books have never been strong on plot, 'Return to Jalna' is more superficial than most of the earlier ones" (12). Most of the reviewers, however, praised the domestic drama lavishly.

XV   Renny's Daughter

Renny's Daughter, (1951) though it offered more of the same brand of domestic crises found in the previous volumes, was partially saved by the comic relief. Miss de la Roche, locked into a family series with set characters and set situations (family gossip at the tea table, triumphs of artistic members of the tribe, small tragedies of the household, enlivened at times with sex), found her way out of her tiresome characters and situations through comic scenes. Low-life comedy was indeed needed, for the plot of the novel would be interesting only to those *voyeurs* who had been spying the antics of the Whiteoaks for a generation.

The world was again about to intrude into life at Jalna, for Mr. Clapperton, that greedy businessman, had again decided to build his model village. Because Renny was adamantly against the project, he could not leave Canada to accompany his beautiful young daughter Adeline to Ireland. On the voyage to Europe, while traveling with her cousin Maurice, who was going to Ireland to claim his estate, and Finch, she fell in love with Maitland Fitzturgis, an impoverished Irish farmer. She spurned the callow Maurice for the thirtyish man-of-the-world Maitland, and she later created a minor scandal in Ireland by running after her reluctant suitor. But Maitland was, alas, not free to marry: he was poor and had the responsibility for an over-talkative mother and an insane sister. Adeline wanted to be engaged, to wait until her lover's situation improved, but he resisted. In England, she learned he had once been married to an actress; but even this news did not diminish the school-girl crush Adeline had on her handsome Irishman.

Meanwhile, Mr. Clapperton was beginning his model village but was losing his wife to the Irish handyman Raikes, he of the smooth tongue and handsome face. Gem, the wife, could hardly be expected to stay in love with the old, crude Clapperton, who kept calling his wife *girlie*. Raikes, a liar and a thief, had completely charmed both the Clappertons; and the old man was too stupid to realize his wife's affections were being stolen. When Clapperton did learn that Raikes had cheated him out of money, he fired the handyman. That night, a carelessly placed cigarette of Raikes ignited Vaughanlands; and Clapperton, in attempting to save a valuable silver service, was killed in the fire. Renny and others who believed Clapperton was a hero, thought he had been attempting to rescue his sister-in-law. Uncle Ernest, excited by the destruction, died peacefully in his sleep; and Adeline and Finch flew home for the funeral. Finch bought Vaughanlands; and the reader knows that Raikes will get possession of Mrs. Clapperton's money.

The plot is banal, but Rags, one of the Whiteoak servants, his fat wife, and Noah Binns, bell ringer and grave digger, are much more prominent in this novel. They give a sense of life to the story. The model village intrusion into Jalna had been played out in other novels, and Adeline's romance is schoolgirlish and tiresome. Noah Binns, a serio-comic character, constantly predicts disaster. In a marvelously conceived scene, he digs a deep grave for Uncle Ernest and is himself unable to get out of it. His Dickensian malapropisms as he conversed with Chalk, the new sexton, are realistic and a perfect demonstration of Miss de la Roche's eye for the comic. Noah, digging the grave, commented (in a Shakesperian fashion) on the Whiteoaks to Chalk:

"Folks like them are gettin' rare. Before long they'll be distinct."

"Extinct," corrected Chalk.

"Have it your own way. That's what young folks is like. They think they know it all. When I feel like givin' a young feller a kick in the pants, I remember I hadn't no sense when I was his age."

It was seldom that Noah Binns was so talkative, but grave digging always exhilarated him. It has been hard indeed for him because of advancing years to give up this profitable pleasure. (248)

The scenes in the kitchen with the Cockney servant Rags and his fat wife, the cook, are also comic. These scenes supply a sense of the vivacious and a gusto for experience missing in the staid, stock characters of the Whiteoaks. Miss de la Roche was indeed a prisoner of those Whiteoaks; though her scenes of comic relief were here more artfully placed than usual in the Jalna stories. For readers who were already devoted fans, however, stock Whiteoak characters were old friends and were accepted.

XVI Variable Winds at Jalna

As a fitting conclusion to the Whiteoak Saga, Miss de la Roche attempted in the last two novels of the series—*Variable Winds at Jalna*, (1954) and *Centenary at Jalna* (1958)—to deal with the perils of marrying Renny's daughter. As usual in most popular fiction, the most difficult situations were overcome in a few sentences. Maitland, the impoverished caretaker of his garrulous mother and insane sister in far away Ireland, sold his farm, his sister recovered her sanity, and all three sailed for the New World, the two women to live in New York, he to take up residence at Jalna, learn about horses, and become Adeline's husband. And the reader was given more than the usual triangle. There was, of course, the wealthy Maurice, still in love with his cousin, and given to alcoholic excesses (like Branwell Brontë) because she cared not for him. And there was Renny himself, in love with his daughter, and she in love with him. Renny found Maitland less than the most desirable son-in-law, for the Irishman cared little about horses. In the Branwell Brontë-Gothic tradition, Maurice went from one alcoholic stupor to another. Maitland (readers knew not to trust handsome Irishmen) began to cast admiring glances toward Roma, Eden's illegitimate daughter.

As one has learned to expect in such novels, the lovers quarreled; and Maitland wearing a swim suit with a hole in the seat, went to the lake with Roma to swim. When Adeline followed them, she saw the two kissing. As was done in biblical times, she stoned those caught in (in this case, symbolic) adultery. Later she described the scene to her father, who was sorry he had not been there to see. The love affair was ended; Maitland, unfaithful lover, was sent away in disgrace. Renny had his daughter back.

Maitland's sister, too, went away under a cloud. She had, after recovering her sanity, had a brief affair in New York; and it was enough to make sensitive artist Finch, who was in love with her, cast her out of his life, at least temporarily. The only happy person was Wakefield, who had started living with Renny's illegitimate daughter, Molly. Maitland, Wakefield told Finch, "convinced me that we were fools to throw away our chances of a happy life because of a legal quibble or some worn-out rule of the Church. He's some years younger than I, but he is more worldly. Perhaps you'd call him hedonistic. Anyhow, I took his advice. Molly was eager to take it" (244-45).

Wakefield had always been a Byronic hero, a descendent of

Wuthering Heights and the Gothic novel. Incest and unusual love affairs were not uncommon themes for Miss de la Roche and for the whole tribe of scribbling women who preceded her —and for those who write for the modern television soap operas. Miss de la Roche did not linger over the implications of incest, as she might have done had she been writing in the 1960's.

One sentimental incident, obviously inspired by Dickens' death scenes, was the final departure of the ninety-eight-year-old Nicholas. Miss de la Roche found it difficult to underplay such Victorian scenes, and it is clear that women readers and viewers have not tired of them in this century.

Aside from the forbidden and, in this case, enjoyed incest, the novel contains little of interest except for three minor characters: Humphrey Bell, Archer Whiteoak, and Dennis Whiteoak. Humphrey Bell (*Bell* was the pen name used by the Brontë sisters) was an impoverished, almost albino young man writing for the popular magazines, radio, and television. He seems to be Miss de la Roche's recollection in tranquility of herself as a young writer. Renny's son, Archer, was a pedantic adolescent, given to Latin quotations. He is comic in much the same way Dr. Bat is in Cooper's *The Prairie*. Archer's world was clearly to be the dry world of scholarship, far away from the Jalna stables. Dennis, Finch's young son, was a sensitive young boy who wanted to cling to his father, just as his mother Sarah had done. Finch, moody, neurotic, temperamental artist that he was, spurned the boy. He was to play a major role in the next novel, *Centenary at Jalna*.

A reviewer in the *New York Times*, November 7, 1954, wrote of *Variable Winds at Jalna*: "Even to be with the Whiteoaks in the midst of distress is somehow comforting; one knows that their sweet-scented world is going to come out all right" (49). *Centenary at Jalna*, which was to follow, was not to be "sweet-scented" at all.

XVII   Centenary at Jalna

Ronald Hambleton argues in his biography of Miss de la Roche that she was capable of artistic development, and he uses as example *Centenary at Jalna* (1958) which was published when she was nearing eighty. It is the character of Dennis which interests him, and he maintains that in this character she was "giving expression to certain motifs of society" (213). Another theory might also be advanced: Miss de la Roche was perhaps attempting to gain new readers by adding large and shocking doses of sadism to her work. In one chapter, "Seen Through A Picture Window," Finch's son, Dennis, who disliked his stepmother, scratched mosquito bites and then stood outside a picture window for his stepmother to see him: "Now she and Dennis were face to face. She saw him raise his arms and extend them, as though on a cross. She saw his bloodstained forehead and the hair in sharp golden points, like thorns. She saw the red prints on the palms of his hands, and the blood on his side. . . .With a strangled cry she repeated his name, then covered her eyes with her hands." The boy then called out, "I'm crucified! Don't you see? I'm crucified!" (64) The scene was not satiric nor was it "black comedy;" as it was seriously presented in the novel, it was violence for its own sake. The rather confused religious imagery was only a mask for sadism.

Dennis was given several similar scenes in the novel. In another scene, his pregnant stepmother started having labor pains; but the boy would not call the doctor, claiming he had forgotten the number. Finally, he did put through a call to the veterinarian, and then ran from the house saying: " 'Go ahead! Have your monster! That's what it is going to be, you know—a monster—a monster. My father doesn't want it—I don't want it—it's yours' " (200).

Miss de la Roche presented other such scenes of cruelty, but she never probed seriously into the problem of evil. She had a good idea in presenting frustrated Dennis, yearning for his father's love, hating the stepmother enough to kill her, detesting the newborn brother enough to almost drown him; but Dennis was not a masterful character study. The confines of the Whiteoak saga kept Miss de la Roche from an intensive study of evil personified. Even his attempted suicide was presented for its shocking qualities, and no real analysis was made of the boy's psychological state.

The main concern in *Centenary at Jalna* was Renny's arranging the marriage of his daughter Adeline to Piers' son Philip;

for if Jalna were once more to be owned by Adeline and Philip, family continuity would be preserved.

The planning of the loveless marriage showed how inverted and incestuous the whole of Jalnaland was. When Renny, for family pride and love of his daughter, spoke to Adeline about such a match, she at first announced she did not wish to marry. Then this scene is described: "He took her in his arms and kissed her trembling lips. 'Not now perhaps, but—the day will come. Then some brute will appear on the scene who will captivate you. . . .' Now her tears were mixed with laughter. They clung together. Noises from the stables reached them, then a sudden shower sounded on the roof and a distant roll of thunder. These sounds enclosed them. They smelled the rain, heard the thunder, and wished for nothing but to be together" (76-77).

Renny had his way. Adeline, with minor protest, went meekly through the charade of marrying a cousin she felt no love for. He was handsome but rather stupid and looked exactly like his great-grandfather Philip; she, all the Whiteoaks declared, was exactly like the old Adeline, though in truth she lacked the character of the grand old lady. In reality, the young Adeline and Philip were to be under the complete domination of her father Renny.

The estate was saved for another generation. Archer, after all, was a Rhodes Scholar with no interest in horses and Jalna. And after that? Miss de la Roche did not seem to see, and certainly her readers did not wish her to describe, the Whiteoaks in decay. But they were; and—though Dennis's murdering of his stepmother, the attempted murder of his half-brother, and his attempted-suicide were somehow glossed over—one knew that a progressive school in New England was not going to be the cure for him. And then there was Wakefield, still trying to bring Molly to his bed again. And there was Renny, perhaps sickest of all the Whiteoaks, who must somehow keep his daughter at Jalna.

XVIII   Farewell to Jalnaland

Ronald Hambleton has argued that the Jalna novels have social significance. He points out that the first volume of Jalna and the Balfour Report (which stated that members of the British Commonwealth were equal) were being written at the same time, and Mr. Hambleton believes that their messages were the same: "British influence had come to an end. I see Gran Whiteoak as typifying the mother country," he goes on, "irascible, touchy, crippled with gout, her brood around her, selfishly clinging to her domain. Most of her brood express the different aspects of Canadian society. Renny, the true heir to British sentiment and tradition; Piers, the Canadian farmer; Augusta, Nicholas, and Ernest—a pas de trois dancing the old regime out; Finch, the despised artist, who comes of age in the late twenties" (220).

It is within the realm of possibility that Miss de la Roche may have, through natural inclination and intuition, arrived at the position ascribed to her by Mr. Hambleton. It is difficult to believe, however, that she thought out her position this carefully. It is true that she admired tradition and fought change; that she was a Royalist and often referred derisively, in her fiction and to friends, to political and social developments in the United States which she found disagreeable.

Lovat Dickson attempted to explain English adulation of Miss de la Roche, and much of what he said applied equally to her American audience:

The Whiteoak books represent the idealized picture of Canada which all English people have. Life is hardly ever painful at Jalna. It's comfortable, it's exciting, there are domestic dramas going on. I think that Englishmen like to believe that anywhere abroad life goes on as it used to go on in England. We always like to think that life for our parents must have been wonderful and life for us is horrid. Englishmen reading about the Whiteoaks think that life is lived that way now, and we know that life is not lived that way in England—nor in Canada.[3] (Quoted in Hambleton, p. 219.)

One could develop the analysis further, for Miss de la Roche's popularity is more complex than Mr. Dickson says. English, American, French, German readers (predominantly women) of the Jalna series found psychological release in stories about slim, hard, virile Renny, a stallion figure. They could feel sympathy for plump Meg, who had been betrayed by her fiancé; readers could pop another bon-bon into their mouths as they read of Meg's secret meals, sign of her suffering. The readers could lose themselves in the colorful world of the dynasty, be amused by and yet admire, the matriarch Adeline, and see her reborn in Renny's daughter. They could follow the progress of the Whiteoak children, cluck over the latest scandal. Jalna novels took the place of gossiping old aunts who told family stories to the accompaniment of rattling family skeletons.

Miss de la Roche did tell her Whiteoak stories well. In spite of her lack of critical theory, she knew how to fill her narratives with sensual details which offered continued entertainment to the masses. And her characters, with their unusual names and individualizing traits were not easily confused in the minds of the reader: Piers and Eden, for example, were such distinct characters that readers need not consult the genealogical chart which accompanied most of the novels. Her chapter headings clearly indicated the movement of her narrative; in *Centenary at Jalna,* for example, the first five chapter headings were these: "Mary Whiteoak's World," "Finch's Return," "The Promising Boy," "In the Basement Kitchen—And After," and "Seen Through A Picture Window." The story moved forward, with no experimentation with time or language; and readers could easily understand what was happening. Miss de la Roche provided entertainment to her readers in almost as painless a fashion as viewing a musical comedy in the movies or a daytime serial on television.

In the serious literary world, however, after first being hailed for *Jalna,* Miss de la Roche was neglected. Although she was not persecuted by Canadian critics, as she intimated in *Ringing the Changes,* serious critics in Canada, in the United States, and in England either ignored her or pointed out the sterility of her presentations of character and life in the seemingly endless Jalna novels and in her other works of the 1930's, 1940's, and 1950's. Many writers in Canada and in other countries undoubtedly admired her as a money-maker, as one who held a large audience; but she was not respected as an artist.

XIX *Two Dramatized Versions of* Jalna

The Whiteoak family was destined for the stage just as Scarlett and Rhett were almost pre-determined to appear in a movie version of *Gone with the Wind.*[4] Just as the possibilities of exploitation in another medium were immediately realized by those around Margaret Mitchell, dramatization of *Jalna* was being suggested as early as 1927. These early proposals languished, for a time, however, until R.K.O. studio bought film rights to *Jalna*, and released the movie version in 1935. The advertising revealed Hollywood's approach to her story: "Brother against brother, bride against bride—family skeleton shakes its bones as young wife comes to stay, and the curious thing we call the family becomes the flaming crucible of love and jealousy, of tragedy and triumph, behind the life-worn walls of Jalna, homestead of the Whiteoaks."[5] Miss de la Roche was reasonably pleased with the adaptation when she first saw it, but in her memoirs she mentioned that her fans were not happy with the casting: "Not one of the attributes that made old Adeline Whiteoak notable belonged to the actress who played the part" (251).

Even before the partial success of the film, *Jalna*, Miss de la Roche had decided to do her own adaptation for the stage. She had written one-act plays in the 1920's, and she was assured that her dialogue in the Jalna novels could be transported almost without revision into the theater. Her dramatization, called *Whiteoaks,* was apparently most amateurish; Mr. Hambleton records that she called for five acts and twelve scene changes, making the play into something of a "pageant" (143). After many London producers had rejected the dramatization, Miss de la Roche approached Nancy Price, producer and actress. Miss Price was interested and eventually played the role of the Grandmother on the stage; but she insisted that the play had to be revised to three acts and one set. With these conditions in mind, and guided by Miss Price, Miss de la Roche rewrote the play; and it opened in 1936. Mr. Hambleton gives an excellent stage history of the production.

The London reviewers were deeply divided. The *Star* wrote after the April 13, 1936, opening: "Very clever of Miss de la Roche not to have made these dull people dull company." The *Daily Telegraph* said: "The author is a good novelist but an immature dramatist. She throws her people on to the stage haphazardly. She does not even explain that the Whiteoaks live in Canada. The play is really too lifelike to be effective, and the presence of a noisy parrot adds to the general confusion."[6]

After a slow start, and mixed reviews, George Bernard Shaw wrote a card to Miss Price: "There's been nothing like it in London since Irving captured it through *The Bells*; and you have left Irving nowhere, and in a horrible hateful play too. But the right sort of stuff all the same. Who is your fiendish collaborator?"[7] Shaw's praise was used in the advertising, with the expected results. Drawing an audience from Miss de la Roche's readers and through word-of-mouth advertising, the play became a success that ran for almost three years.

The touring company had much less success in the United States. John Mason Brown wrote, "My own suspicion is New York will not be able to take *Whiteoaks* to its heart as London has done for the simple reason that there is no play to take."[8] Canadian reviewers, however, were much more enthusiastic. But Miss de la Roche did not care for Ethel Barrymore's interpretation of Adeline Whiteoak; she preferred Nancy Price's performance.

The play and its success were of great importance to Miss de la Roche; she gave it a chapter in her memoirs and quoted with relish St. John Ervine's review in the *Observer:* "This piece. . . is easily one of the best plays now running in London. If the author were Chekhov and the principal part were played by Mr. Gielgud, all the fashion-followers would be cramming themselves into the Playhouse to see it" (272).

Little, Brown and Company published the script of *Whiteoaks* in 1936, and from that text it is clear that Miss de la Roche had been forced to restrain her multiplication of characters and events from the first two Jalna novels—*Jalna* and *Whiteoaks of Jalna*—which she used together to make the one play. Eden, the poet, disappeared, as well as his wife Alayne; as a result, the Renny-Alayne and Eden-Pheasant affairs need not be introduced. Instead, the play concentrated more on eating and family quarrels. The first act, like many another British play or its close imitation, was devoted to a meal; and one can wring a good deal of domestic drama from the pouring of the tea and the eating of a soufflé.

If plot there was in the first two acts of this play, it was what was to happen to the old Grandmother's fortune when she died. And die she did, on stage, as she played backgammon at the end of Act II. Act III can then be an account of the beastly family quarrel after it was known that Finch had inherited the fortune. The bickering perhaps gave the audience a feeling of the reality of Miss de la Roche's world; but the play was, as were most of the novels, without style, grace, or wit.

The strong-willed old Grandmother made the play appear more interesting than it was, but *Whiteoaks,* though a stage success, is without literary merit. Both the movie and the play undoubtedly helped sell many more Jalna books.

CHAPTER 4

Critics and Fans of Jalnaland

When *Jalna* appeared in 1927, with all the fanfare of the ten thousand dollar prize, reviews in the United States were, as expected, generally favorable. Marie Luhrs, in the *Nation* for November 16, 1927, wrote what might be considered a standard notice: "It is beautiful, engrossing, and unusual—a novel whose interest and action flow out of its extremely live characters and gorgeous scenery." Even those who had reservations were mild in their criticism; for example, Miriam Colgate in the *Bookman* for September, 1927, noted, "The faults of the book are faults of generosity—too much material, too many characters, an embarrassment of incident."

I *Jalna Novels and the Reviewers*

Miss de la Roche was an overnight public figure in Canada, and this account of a dinner in her honor in Toronto in May, 1921, indicates the kind of publicity she was then receiving, publicity which undoubtedly helped sell *Jalna* in Canada:

In proposing the toast, "Our Guest of Honor," Dr. Charles G. D. Roberts spoke of the honor which the gifted young author had brought not only to her native city but to all Canadian writers.

Miss de la Roche's simple response delighted everyone. . . Miss de la Roche said she found that winning a prize was a very wonderful experience, but one that required perfect mental balance.

. . . .

In proposing the toast to "The Arts in Education," Sir Robert Falconer, President of the University of Toronto, said that he had been struck by the simplicity and sincerity of Miss de la Roche's words on this occasion, and that he had noticed these same qualities in the first instalment of "Jalna"; they were the two essential qualities of all great art. The speaker drew attention to Canada's geographical position in the very centre of the civilized world, and pointed out that this author's achievement was all the more impressive because she had been measured with the best of other countries.[1]

Mr. Hambleton has shown that the English were reserved at first; the book did not sell well. *The Times Literary Supplement* for December 1, 1927, noted: "The reader's sympathies and interests are too much divided to become very deep, and in spite of all its striking qualities the book remains in some ways ineffective." Though Hodder and Stoughton, who published the book, advertised extensively in *The Times Literary Supplement* during the fall of 1927, the company did not mention *Jalna.*

When *Whiteoaks of Jalna* appeared two years later, reviews were still extremely favorable; but, as is usually the case, several reviewers thought the sequel was not so good as the original. The *Nation and Atheneum* for December 7, 1929, found that the description of Finch's attempted suicide was "disappointing" and that Miss de la Roche "scarcely follows up its psychological consequences."

When the next novel—*Finch's Fortune*—appeared, the critics could not refrain from comparing Miss de la Roche with John Galsworthy. M. M. Waterman in the *Bookman* for November, 1931, said, "Like the Forsyte Saga, the story of Jalna can go on and on, and the Whiteoak enthusiast hopes that Miss de la Roche will keep up her series." R. B. Macdougall in *The Saturday Review of Literature* for October 3, 1931, who also took up the Forsyte theme, argued that *Jalna* was inferior to the Galsworthy series because the Forsytes were "inextricably bound up with the whole of English life" while the Whiteoaks were isolated from Canadian life.

Miss de la Roche might well have stopped with a Jalna trilogy, but her readers and her publishers wanted more Whiteoak stories. From the time of the first Jalna novel, she began to receive letters begging her to continue the Whiteoak chronicle. How many authors, newly made rich, would be able to turn against the chance of greater riches, to risk losing loyal readers? For example, Lloyd C. Douglas wrote this fan letter soon after *Jalna* appeared: "Jalna is the best novel since 'The Way of All Flesh.' " He suggested, as many of her readers did, "We will look for the sequel with high anticipation."[2]

The readers remained ecstatic, and most of the reviews during the 1930's, 1940's, and 1950's were unvarying. As each new novel appeared, a few nay-sayers found the latest installment somewhat more creaking than the first; but the majority of critics summarized the plot briefly and recommended the novel. For example, in the *Christian Science Monitor* for May 22, 1958, N. E. Taylor in reviewing *Centenary at Jalna* asserted that Miss de la Roche had spread Canada's fame throughout the world and that "Jalna has become synonymous with Canada" (13). The anonymous reviewer in *The Times Literary Supplement*, July 25, 1958, summarized another, more critical position: "For addicts, all the familiar ingredients are there. . . But for anyone who refuses to be dazzled. . . the behaviour of some of the adult members of the Whiteoaks family appears unbelievably obtuse and stupid" (421).

But by the time this review appeared, Miss de la Roche had long since lost her *Times Literary Supplement* readers. In fact, one gets an extremely narrow view of Miss de la Roche's appeal and acclaim if one reads the reviews in the respectable, well-established newspapers and journals which are indexed or which are sampled by *Book Review Digest*. Macmillan's of London kindly permitted an examination of its scrapbooks containing English and Commonwealth reviews of Miss de la Roche's works; these made it evident that the provincial English newspapers and journals for women constantly gave her books brief but favorable notices. The clipping book, for example, has thirty reviews and notices of *Mary Wakefield*. These two, from women's magazines, are also typical of the provincial newspaper notices.

In *Everywoman*, February, 1950, one finds the following commentary: "All Mazo de la Roche's Whiteoaks novels tell rattling good stories; all their characters are bursting with vitality. The latest, *Mary Wakefield*, which fits in between *The Building of Jalna* and *Young Renny*, is well up to standard. Mary's a governess—but a young lady of character and of passion well spent." And in *Modern Woman*, March, 1950: "Another of Miss de la Roche's popular 'Jalna' novels, and there is no doubt people do like to have a family they can go on reading about. This time the story is about a charming young English girl who goes out to Canada as governess to the tumultuous Whiteoaks spriglings who live in the house called Jalna. A nice novel for a cosy afternoon."

These two notices indicate that the journals knew that the English housewife needed escape from the drudgery of her life, wanted to read of glamorous estate life in Canada, needed diversion during the long afternoons. The provincial papers constantly spoke of the "well-loved family," of the delight in meeting familiar characters once again. The *Smith Trade News* of May 1, 1954, however, spoke of more practical matters: "Faithful fans will be eager to buy this to add to other volumes in the Whiteoak canon on their shelves. There should be a big demand at libraries." Obviously a certain kind of reader did "collect" the Jalna novels. These novels were also, as this review indicates, staples in the light reading sections of public and lending libraries.

Continuing good notices in many leading newspapers and journals in England and America must have pleased Miss de la Roche, but the brief notes and summaries in provincial papers and in women's publications were of more importance to her sales. The good ladies of her audience needed to know that Miss de la Roche had written another saga; then they would buy it or borrow it from a library. After *Jalna*, Miss de la Roche lost her sophisticated—perhaps one should more properly say semi-sophisticated—readers. Certainly after 1930, her audience was definitely "lowbrow."

When the Jalna novels first appeared, the advertising was directed toward several groups. Atlantic-Little, Brown, in its constant references to the ten thousand dollar award, courted the Babbitts who would be impressed by prize money. *The Atlantic Monthly*, though it had intellectual pretensions, helped publicize *Jalna* by serializing it in issues from May through October of 1927. The first notice of the novel and its author in "The Contributor's Column" spoke of the eleven hundred manuscripts in the contest and Miss de la Roche's winning by a unanimous vote of the judges. The ten thousand dollar prize was featured, as if this were an indication of the worth of the novel. The note in the May, 1927, issue said of Miss de la Roche: "First a writer of whimsical juveniles, she now comes into her own as a novelist of bold and original power" (716).

Miss de la Roche clearly did not need a press agent, for in the

June, 1927, issue of *The Atlantic Monthly* "The Contributor's Column" carried a puff about her intended to arrest the attention of readers and prospective readers: "As her name indicates, she is of French descent. One of her royalist ancestors was guillotined in the Revolution. 'Since then,' she says, 'we have been notable only for our improvidence' " (869). Walter Winchell would not have been embarrassed to carry such an exotic account in his gossip column. In the July, 1927, issue of the magazine, "The Contributor's Column" announced that, once the "applause subsides," Miss de la Roche and her adopted sister would retreat to the woods, "whence, rumor has it, a sequel is to be forthcoming." Before *Jalna* had even appeared, Miss de la Roche's publishers were busy paving the way for another best-selling novel.

The August, 1927, issue of *The Atlantic Monthly* again used gossip to spread her fame. It reported that, when Miss de la Roche was on her way to her summer cottage, the car she and Miss Clement were in was caught "between the closed gates of a railroad crossing" and the two ladies had to jump to escape the oncoming train. Then, to stimulate additional public clamor for another Whiteoaks novel, the gossip continued: "Miss de la Roche is contemplating a sequel to 'Jalna,' but this is, we believe, far too hazardous a way of collecting material, however exciting." To hold the interest of new subscribers, the magazine then ran a summary of the action of the parts of the novel previously published.

The September, 1927, issue of *The Atlantic Monthly* published a begging letter to Miss de la Roche from a mechanic in Louisiana. The man, a native of Belgium, announced, "I am finishing my invention who will save *Millions, Millions* to U. S. and I *hope* Canada will get her shares about it." He was obviously not about to explain the nature of his invention, but he needed eighty-five dollars to get a patent, and he would pay her compound interest if she would send the money. The letter was obviously intended to demonstrate that Miss de la Roche was already a celebrity.

Building on all this free publicity in *The Atlantic Monthly*, Little, Brown and Company purchased large advertisements for *Jalna*. In *The Saturday Review of Literature*, for October 8, 1927, for instance, the Little, Brown advertisement showed the book's dust jacket, with the $10,000 prize emblazoned on it, a drawing of a birch tree being blown by a strong wind, and a picture of Miss de la Roche, with bobbed hair, looking young and flapperish. Then the advertisement listed praise from "Five Leading Novelists": Gertrude Atherton, Honoré Willsie Morrow, Margaret Prescott Montague, Basil King, and Sir Gilbert Parker. Little, Brown obviously had its own secret definition of "Leading Novelists" (177).

In the October 29th issue of *The Saturday Review of Literature* the Little, Brown advertisement quoted a few words from reviews: " 'An achievement.' *New York Times Book Review.*" " 'Robust and brawny fiction. Energetic. Alive.' *Time.*" This advertisement also featured a small woodcut of young-looking Miss de la Roche gazing admiringly at a small dog. If the dog lovers of America would read *Jalna*, Little, Brown would clearly have one of the best sellers of all times (257).

The November 26, 1927, advertisement in *The Saturday Review of Literature* announced that Jalna "leads the latest list of fiction best sellers. . . .*85th Thousand Already*" (345). In the December 10 issue of the same magazine, Little, Brown published the same advertisement, with a new figure on sales: "100th Thousand Already!" (431). After the Christmas sales period was over, advertising dwindled in *The Saturday Review of Literature*, but on February 11, 1928, a Little, Brown advertisement noted that *Jalna* was "The best seller for the third consecutive month," with 110,000 copies in print (595). In the "Spring Number" of April 21, 1928, the publisher's advertisement did not feature *Jalna* but said, "Wherever you go you will hear people discussing 'Jalna,' the Atlantic $10,000 prize novel. If you haven't read it you won't be able to take part. Now in its 125th thousand" (789). The advertising campaign was highly effective, and Miss de la Roche was well aware that much of the success of the novel was due to it.

Whiteoaks of Jalna appeared in late summer in time for vacation readers but late enough to be also advertized for Christmas buying. An advertisement in *The Saturday Review of Literature* of September 21, 1929, emphasized that the novel was the sequel to *Jalna*, a ten thousand dollar prize novel, in case anyone had forgotten. The same woodcut of Miss de la Roche and the dog was published, along with a new letter of praise from "famous novelist" Gertrude Atherton: "I found 'Whiteoaks of Jalna' even more interesting than 'Jalna,' and no one could say more than that. To my mind those are two of the finest novels ever published in America" (164). The advertisement noted that forty-five thousand copies were in print, and the publishers undoubtedly thought that a testimonial from Mrs. Atherton, author of that *succès de scandale, Black Oxen*, would boost sales even higher.

As the Christmas season approached, the sequel continued to sell well and was much advertised. By October 12, fifty-five thousand copies were in print, according to the advertisement in *The Saturday Review of Literature*, and in the Christmas book issue of December 7, 1929, the novel was one of twelve recommended books on the Little, Brown list, with sixty-five thousand copies then in print (515). The publishers were not advertising so forcefully as they had done two years before, and the new novel was clearly not selling so well. No doubt the publishers expected word-of-mouth advertising to be important, and they also may have counted on the readers' memories of Miss de la Roche's earlier success to lead them to part willingly with their money again. Readers were expected to become addicted, to look forward to the almost yearly Whiteoaks novel just as radio fans looked forward in the 1930's to the daily installment of *Ma Perkins*.

As an indication of how the advertising changed, when *Variable Winds at Jalna* appeared in 1954, the Little, Brown advertisement in the New York *Herald Tribune Book Review* for November 14 gave the novel a prominent place, but one subservient to J. P. Marquand's *Thirty Years*. The advertisement reproduced a picture of the dust jacket of Miss de la Roche's new novel—a romantic view of the manor house. The advertising copy writer insisted that "every scene is sparked with surprise and drama, with the joys and sorrows and discontents and abiding satisfactions that are the true dimensions of family life." No mention was made of numbers of copies sold.

The appeal by the advertising writers was more pointed in the Chicago *Sunday Tribune Magazine of Books* on June 8, 1958. The Little, Brown advertisement for *Centenary at Jalna* appeared under the heading "Delight for Summer Reading." The writer stressed the novel's universal appeal, or rather its large

[105]

number of readers, and gave enough of the plot to drive one to the bookstore: "Millions of readers the world over have followed the fortunes of the beloved Whiteoak family through the years. In her new novel, Mazo de la Roche carries her famous saga into the mid-1950's, and to that summer day when the boisterous and fiercely loyal family gather to celebrate the hundredth anniversary of the old homestead. . ." (7). The tone was meant to entice Illinois and other Midwestern ladies seeking light summer reading; it invited commoners everywhere to participate in the festivities of the landed gentry.

II *Miss de la Roche's English-speaking Fans*

Miss de la Roche was clearly influenced by the thousands of fan letters she received, for they reassured her that she was writing what her audience wanted to read and told her that her fans wanted more of the same. (These letters, which number into the thousands, form a unique collection in the Department of Rare Books and Special Collections of the University of Toronto.) The early letters were often from well-educated men and women. A Radcliffe student, studying for a doctoral degree, wrote in 1927 that she was reading the serialization of *Jalna* in *The Atlantic Monthly.* She felt "impelled" to write: "There is a delicacy and subtlty [*sic*] of keen perception and sympathetic human understanding throughout it all that I am sure could be attained only in this psychologically-curious twentieth century of ours—whether you choose to admit personally any interest in it or not."

A Canadian reader gave Miss de la Roche a symbolic cultural/political reading of the novel in 1927. He was pleased with the satire and the characters. Of the Grandmother he wrote,

senile, repulsive and grinning. . .there she sits—old Canada arrogant, greedy Georgian, propped up by lazy, narrow-minded Victorian loyalty, and sapping the very life of the frustrated young of her land.

By all means, Miss de la Roche, write a sequel, another work of art and genius, and kill her off.

This is a mighty task.

And Miss de la Roche complied. After *Jalna*, however, her

intellectual fan-letter writers largely deserted her, but hundreds of her other admirers did not. The following letter, complete with underscorings, is typical of the many she continued to receive:

I just had to pour out my sentiments to *you* the most logical person. Never before have I so greedily devoured anything—such a family—they're *real*—they capture the imagination—you *must* love them—your names are so vastly intriguing—I shall never forget *one member* of the delicious clan—and I implore you to tell us more about Finch—what of little Wakefield—and Renny and Alayne—its [*sic*] the most delightful sensation in the world to feel on such intimate terms with each of them—one can hardly be kept from entering their very hearts and lives—My friends and I discuss the Whiteoaks with much the same interest and zest that marks our conversations about mutual friends and relatives—particularly those in whom we feel a *more* then passing concern.

Though the style of the fan letters was often as gushing as this one was, most letters were generally grammatically correct and neatly written. Miss de la Roche's fans wanted to make the best impression on a Famous Author.

One lady from Canada reported in 1954 a kind of psychic experience; the Jalna novels were the medium she used to feel close to her dead mother:

Your books have spoiled me for any others. I just read the Whiteoak series over and over again. How I adore Finch! How I love them all! . . . My mother also loved the Whiteoaks. She read all but the "Whiteoak Brothers" before she died, and I had the feeling she was beside me as I read this latest.

My husband laughs at me when I've finished one of your books. I've got to hug it to me before putting it away.

From Wales, a reader apparently in ill health and suffering from the anxieties of wartime life in Britain, wrote in 1941: "At a time like the present—it is difficult to get books which provide one with the necessary respite from tension and anxiety—but your books have proved a God-send to me, and I only hope, I shall be able to read some more of them. . . ." This letter indicates how the Whiteoak series provided an escape from the horrors of one's existence, an escape to a much simpler, uncluttered world, one isolated from the stress of modern life. This Welsh fan also addressed her letter to "Dear Sir," a common mistake found in many other letters in the de la Roche collection in the University of Toronto Library.

Some of the letters strike one as having come from households fully as bizarre as those described in the novels themselves. This letter was obviously carefully worded to attract the attention of Miss de la Roche:

'The Whiteoaks of Jalna' has just passed thru our family like an epidemic of measles, before one of us was through with it the next one was down with it—but, unlike measles, we have all enjoyed it very much.

But we can't bear not to know what Finch does with his money—We, like the rest of your reading public, will be waiting anxiously for the book which we know must follow. When can we expect it?

The closing remarks and signatures suggest a drama which would have interested Sherwood Anderson:

Very truly yours,
An Ordinary American Family
   consisting of
Mrs.   and
Her husband, Mr.   , and
Her twin brother, Mr.   , and
His wife, Mrs.
   All living at
      Avenue,   , Ohio.

One wonders whether Miss de la Roche reflected on the inner lives of this "Ordinary American Family." Did she find in them living proof that families actually had such tangled personal relations as her Jalna creations did?

One literary-worshiping lady saw Miss de la Roche as novelist turned prophet. She wrote to her literary *guru* in 1933: "We have built a shrine in our home around the name of Mazo de la Roche and her books which give us a true picture of life and also the soul of life."

Interestingly enough, Miss de la Roche's readers did not comment on the sex and sadism in the novels. In fact, they often spoke of the novels' wholesome qualities. One reader from Massachusetts announced in a letter that she was having her fourteen-year-old daughter read the novels in chronological order. The fan then asserted that, "In view of the trashy, sensual literature that is in our bookstores and libraries for our young people to read, a book or series of books like the Jalna series is not only a real treat, but they are books which one remembers, and more important, they are books one isn't ashamed to put into the hands of their teen-agers." Miss de la Roche *was* discrete in her sex and sadism; she would never be so explicit as Grace Metalious of *Peyton Place*, and the Puritans rarely found fault with the Whiteoaks, even when they had extramarital affairs, illegitimate children, or committed incest.

One can categorize many types of English-speaking fans who wrote to her: lonely widows writing from their sickbeds, isolated ranch and farm wives, middle-aged housewives no longer needed to look after young children and seeking escape through fiction from household chores, the unemployed during the 1930's who hadn't the price of a movie ticket, and teen-aged girls. Many such readers bragged about how many times they had read each novel, just as many movie fans wrote Margaret Mitchell of seeing *Gone with the Wind* fifty times.

Variations in the fan letters show some of Miss de la Roche's special appeal beyond these categories. A woman from New York, writing in 1931, indicated her own sexual fantasies: "My father was a philanderer and like Renny he would never stoop to lie about it. You and I know, I think, that such a man makes a wonderful father, wins the love of all who know him. So often it isn't brought out as a virtue. . . .I overlooked that when I married. I have a husband who wouldn't dream of looking at another woman, and there are actually times, Mazo, that I wish he would." One may infer from the letter that the reader was quite willing to conjure red-haired, virile Renny into her own bed. Miss de la Roche's sexual scenes obviously must have been of great comfort to many of the readers, but most were too repressed to refer to their fantasies.

One Puritanically inclined lady, who found the Wakefield-Molly relationship rather startling, wrote that it "seems almost like incest, even though they are not married—is it not a punishable offence?" Miss de la Roche's reply is not extant, but the philosophical question is an amusing one: would the affair not have been incestuous had they somehow gone through a marriage ceremony? It is clear that the correspondent felt the wedding ceremony had some magical, protective quality.

Many of the readers wrote extremely long letters, giving

their family histories and often enclosing snapshots. Some fans, knowing that Miss de la Roche was a dog fancier, enclosed pictures of their own pets. Several readers wanted to know the exact location of Jalna. One Southern reader, planning a Canadian vacation, wanted precise information on how to reach the estate; she was puzzled that the descriptions of the location in the novels were always vague.

Even in the 1950's, readers were asking Miss de la Roche to fill in some gap in her story. They often provided a suitable plot: the marriage of two of the characters, for example. Others, more interested in a dramatized version, suggested leading actors and actresses for roles. Many readers recognized as early as 1927 the possibility of turning *Jalna* into a play or movie, and several aspiring dramatists wrote saying they were actually at work on such a version.

One of the most amusing of these letters proposed a transvestite version of the play. A Canadian fan in 1933 wrote that he had been wanting to do a dramatization of the "old war horse, Gran" and had sent copies of the first two Jalna volumes to the actor George Arliss, who was then searching for a suitable vehicle. Mr. Arliss, the fan thought, should take the role of Adeline Whiteoak. The fan hastily added a justification for such unusual casting:

And here I would interpolate that, after many heated discussions with a bookish friend. . .as to the vexed question of it being considered infra dig' for an actor to interpret a feminine role, versus my contention that an "old war-horse" who is about to become a centenarian may quite properly be considered as sexless, I gradually accepted the fact that my viewpoint was probably unorthodox, in that Mr. Arliss (while acknowledging the books as a source of much pleasure to both him and Mrs. Arliss) made no reference to having seen a possibility for himself in the part of Gran.

After George Arliss did not cast himself in the role of Gran Whiteoak, the fan saw a movie with Marie Dressler and immediately decided she could be cast in the role of the grandmother. Not only did the fan act as casting agent, he decided to be his own scenario writer and set to work (without permission) fashioning a script from the first two novels in the series. Miss de la Roche's reply is not available, but she obviously had to explain copyright law to the fan.

A graduate student from Yugoslavia studying at a large American university wrote in 1930 that he had written his memoirs, primarily dealing with his wartime experiences in the Balkan Wars of 1912-13 and in World War I, but that his manuscript needed some editorial work. He offered to give her one-third of the royalties and "an expression of thanks in the preface of the book" for her help. The help was not forthcoming, but Miss de la Roche received several other requests of a similar nature. Obviously, these correspondents felt that, if she could write best sellers, she could edit best sellers, thereby increasing the wealth of both parties involved.

III   *Foreign Fans of the Whiteoaks*

A few readers from non-English-speaking countries began writing to Miss de la Roche after *Jalna* first appeared, but her volume of mail increased after her novels were translated. According to one press release in the scrapbooks in Macmillan's London office, the Whiteoak books were translated into French, Swedish, Danish, Norwegian, Dutch, German, Hungarian, Czech, Finnish, Polish, Spanish, Portuguese, and Italian. According to Ronald Hambleton, there were authorized translations into sixteen languages, as well as numerous cases of pirating (50-51).

Though Miss de la Roche's early Continental readers knew English, their written English was somewhat stiff; and they often wrote expressing their enjoyment of the novels in much the same way this Swiss reader did: "I loved them [the Jalna novels] so much that since I have finished them, I feel as if dear friends, in whose lives I am deeply interested, had left me. I am missing them." The reader then stated that she had wanted to translate the novels into German but had just discovered the translation had just been made.

After the war, the tone of the letters from Continental readers rather abruptly changed. One Dutch reader wrote in 1947:

Dear Sir (Madam?) As one of your readers of your "Chronicles of the Whiteoak Family," I am so grateful to you for the pleasure you have given me through your most interesting books, that I simply cannot help thanking you, also in the name of a great many Dutch people who enjoyed them as much as myself. In the last year of the war, when we had no light, no gas, no water and hardly any food, when everything of culture was forbidden by our oppressors and we could not get hold of any books worth reading, a friend of mine came to see me. She was quite excited and told me, that she had got six volumes of a series of novels treating 3 generations of one family, the White-oaks. . . .

Many other readers wrote that their wartime reading of the Jalna novels brought them into contact with an English democratic tradition which they were officially forbidden to discuss. A German woman, a patient in a Heidelberg hospital not long after the war, wrote:

I think that you did so much more for peace than any politicians can do—as far as peace is based on the feelings among people. . . .

As for us Germans sitting in a trap there is no other possibility for learning about foreigners than by books. . . .I suppose with more knowledge about other nations Germans wouldn't have become so narrow-sighted. . .so self-possessed and intolerant as one is with such a small mental horizon.

Excuse me—you certainly know well enough what is the trouble with us Germans—though I hope you don't feel too antagonistic.

One is tempted to imagine Miss de la Roche as a Canadian delegate to the United Nations.

After translations began to appear, housewives in Continental countries took to the novels in much the same fashion as housewives in England and America. One can judge something about the letter of a French correspondent from this penciled reply by Miss de la Roche:

Dear Madame: I am happy to receive your delightful letter and to know that the chronicles of the Whiteoaks have given you so much pleasure. Your letter is one which I shall cherish, and I thank you for writing to me.

I shall tell my publishers of your suggestion for a map of the neighborhood of Jalna but indeed many other readers have asked for the same thing and still my publishers appear to think it is not necessary.

I am glad that you found the latest volume as interesting as the others and hope before very long to write of further developments in the lives of the Whiteoaks.

It is clear, then, that Miss de la Roche took her fan letters seriously and replied in a way which would certainly assure the continued interest of the reader. At the end of the letter just quoted was a request that the letter be translated into French. Obviously the French housewife had read a translation, and a reply in French was required. To another French reader, Miss de la Roche wrote:

Letters from readers in France are among my most cherished. And when they tell me that my characters are sympathetic and alive to them it brings all the more pleasure.

You must not feel that it was a waste of my time to read your letter, as I most appreciate your kindness in writing.

Indeed, whatever her feelings were, Miss de la Roche did answer her fan letters. Several letters to her mentioned replies to earlier ones.

IV *A Gentle Rebuke*

Amazingly, few readers wrote to complain about the subject matter or the style of writing in the Jalna novels; but Miss de la Roche may not have kept most of the letters critical of her writing. Two readers did notice that Miss de la Roche wrote "Dutch Fraulein" when she actually should have written "German Fraulein"; but, in general, her readers were not so critical. One gentleman, writing from Chicago in 1935, did raise some serious questions: the characters in the Jalna novels, he asserted, "all seem to be living in the past. Not a single one of them expresses an intelligent idea on the problems of our day and their possible solution. In other words, they have shut themselves off from the world, shirking their duties towards it, much as a truant child might stay away from school, as it feels itself incompetent to do the lessons expected of it."

Miss de la Roche's readers (or those who wrote to her) did not appear to agree with the Chicago gentleman; they wanted to escape into the isolated Jalna Playland.

V *The de la Roche Fan Letter Collection*

The letters in the de la Roche collection in the University of Toronto Library are fascinating for the light they shed on popular taste. They have been quoted from at great length; for large collections of fan letters to writers have not previously been readily available. The great public adulation for Dickens and Scott has often been written about, but the actual letters of the public have been lost.

Miss de la Roche was clearly captive of her own fantasy world, her publishers, and her public. She had no delusions about the "importance" of her Jalna novels; she remarked in 1935 in a letter quoted by Hambleton:

. . .I do agree that the Whiteoak books are not important in the sense of carrying a "message." I am not drawn to writing long psychological novels which, after six months, one can usually buy from the bargain counter for two shillings.

I myself think that merely the wide-spread interest in the Whiteoak family makes them important (17).

She did not realize that she was writing "psychological novels," but the statement shows clearly that she did not delude herself by thinking of the Jalna novels as great works of art. Her concern was to write novels which would continue to sell and not be remaindered, and she considered herself as fulfilling a public need when she created a fictional family that was of widespread interest to readers.

But the question remains: was she aware of what makes the readers interested? Clearly she had several groups of readers. Lonely ranchers' wives in Wyoming and teen-aged girls in Canberra found the novels appealing in different ways. For the frustrated woman, hungering for a virile male, Miss de la Roche could offer Renny, who smelled of the stables but was found irresistible by the neighboring ladies. For high-school girls, she could offer escape into a fantasy world far different from dull parents and staid schools. For garden-club types, yearning after culture, she offered various artistic types: Finch, the musician; Eden, the poet; and Wakefield, actor and playwright—three artists idealized and exaggerated. The culturally hungry could feel they had partaken of some of the so-called glamor of the bohemian world. Philistines, on the other hand, could feel superior, but at the same time they could relish descriptions of Eden's troubled life, his affair with Pheasant, his losing his first wife to Renny, his illegitimate daughter. Philistines could cluck over Wakefield's incestuous attachment to Renny's natural daughter, and they could be properly aroused by Finch's sadistic son and by the horrible deaths of Finch's wives.

Miss de la Roche presented the nineteenth-century stereotypes of artists, images still in favor with the great reading public. Artists should suffer (for the romantically inclined reader): Finch and Eden both had tuberculosis, a proper artistic illness good enough for Keats, Emerson, Thoreau, and Camille. Artists should also be somewhat balmy: Finch, misunderstood by the horsy set, had severe attacks of nerves, was forever moody, and attempted suicide. Readers of a certain age and temperament no doubt could feel that they would be the perfect mother for him; they could protect him from the cruelty of the world and, in protecting him, allow him to "create."

For the tradition-minded, Miss de la Roche offered a close-knit family, one in which members were constantly lashing one another verbally, but one which presented a united front to the world. Traditionalists could also retreat from the present by escaping into the past. Her Jalna novels, whether set in the nineteenth or twentieth century, pictured a simplistic world known best to those at home in the soapland of radio and television serials.

The hankering of the urban dweller for the simple agricultural life (especially on an estate or plantation) is a common yearning of the reader of escape fiction. Miss de la Roche rarely broke her rural spell. Although she at times moved the action briefly to New York or England, it was clear that she and her characters were not comfortable there, and back they would go to Jalna.

For readers wanting sex and sadism, Miss de la Roche was obliging, though she never said that she did so deliberately; she never admitted that one or two provocative scenes in each novel may have been calculated to increase sales. Family scandal *did* erupt in each Jalna novel, though the scandal never really injured seriously the reputation of the Anglo-Saxon Whiteoaks. Still, each novel had its socially acceptable, or socially deplored, love making. Several volumes had elements of cruelty, though these scenes were not numerous enough to make the readers begin to whisper that the author was an evil-minded old woman. Perhaps one characteristic that saved Miss de la Roche's reputation was her constant habit of presenting erotic scenes in a schoolgirlish, naïve way. In *Return to Jalna,* for example, she dramatized a primitive sexual fear: Piers returned from World War II minus a leg; and, on his first night home, he placed Pheasant's hand on the stump of his leg:

"Is it going to make you feel different toward me?" he whispered.

"Oh, Piers, how can you?" . . . She bent and pressed her trembling lips against the maimed limb. "My precious love!"

He said sternly—"I don't mean because of any hero stuff. I mean because of my value—as a man."

"That's what I mean too!" she cried eagerly. "I mean as a man" (105).

Miss de la Roche, always intent on giving the public what it wanted, was also willing to exploit history. In *Morning at Jalna,* her last and perhaps worst novel, she added the American Civil War to her saga, no small feat since even southern Ontario is a long way from the South. As usual, the blurb writer for Pan Books caught just the right tone: "The year is 1863, and across the Canadian border the American Civil War is in full course. Into the peaceful world of Jalna come two mysterious and fascinating visitors from the Southern States, Curtis Sinclair and his elegant wife, Lucy. Are they fugitives? or are they something infinitely more exciting and, even, dangerous—secret agents of the South plotting to harass the Northern Government from the neutral ground of the Whiteoak homestead?" Miss de la Roche here, however, could hardly give the public what it wanted; it was hard to burn Atlanta from Ontario. Her attempt to exploit the Civil War was a complete fiasco.

To those readers unable or unwilling to grapple with the subtleties of a Henry James, or a James Joyce, Miss de la Roche offered an easy-to-read story and strong characterizations. Frank Luther Mott in *Golden Multitudes* quoted Dorothy Canfield Fisher, who was a member of the board of selection for the Book-of-the-Month Club: "By and large, what readers seem to like to find in a book is contact with living, vital personalities" (288). Miss de la Roche's imagination, her playing the Play, developed her ability to present such seemingly alive personalities, and her readers obviously felt she had succeeded. As Professor Mott showed in his chapter "Is There A Best Seller Formula?" vividness, sentiment, even sentimentality, and sensationalism are important elements in the best seller; and Miss de la Roche obviously supplied all of these.

Miss de la Roche was interested in telling a story, and her prose was a means to this end. She obviously did not labor over her style, did not experiment, did not strive for organic imagery. She concentrated on a lively narrative and concerned herself with characters and episodes which held the reader's attention. Her readers clearly approved of her approach to literature. Over twelve million copies of the Whiteoak volumes (according to Pan) have been sold; it is evident that Miss de la Roche found the key to popular success and that she fulfilled a public need. She entertained a huge audience.

CHAPTER 5

Away From Jalnaland

E VEN after *Jalna*, Miss de la Roche's success with non-Whiteoak fiction and non-fiction was not what she hoped for.
Her short stories and novels, children's stories and autobiogra-
phies were published; and some readers, no doubt out of loyalty, did buy and read them, reviewers did take notice of them,
but the reception was generally cool. Miss de la Roche was fond
of some of these failures, and thought they were quite well done,
but none of them were artistic achievements; they were not the
great works of art popular writers often say they *really* want to be
producing, if only they were not forced to write what the public
wanted.

I *Fiction:* Lark Ascending

The first non-Whiteoak novel after *Jalna* was *Lark Ascending*
(1932), which was composed in England. Miss de la Roche was
often depressed while working on it, she says in her memoirs,
because Ellery Sedgwick, her *Atlantic* mentor, disapproved of
the setting. When the novel appeared, Little, Brown, and Company saw fit to list Miss de la Roche's publications opposite the
title page. The titles they included are rather curious: the three
Jalna novels previously published, plus "A Fourth Volume in
Preparation," *Low Life and Other Plays*, and *Portrait of a Dog. Explorers of the Dawn, Possession,* and *Delight*
which had been brought out by other publishers, are missing;
Little, Brown probably did not wish to help competitors, but
they also appeared to want Miss de la Roche to be thought of in
a special way: as creator of the Whiteoaks ("Don't worry

[119]

folks, you will have another Jalna novel soon"), as author of a dog book certain to appeal to pet lovers everywhere, and, to add a slightly exotic note, as playwright. Special images help sell special books; in this case, the new novel by an already established best-selling author needed some special help. Would the ladies, slavering to read more about Renny, tolerate a fictional work not devoted to the Whiteoaks? The publisher seemed to be uncertain and felt the need to give an extra boost to the cause of sales and profits.

Miss de la Roche obviously tried hard not to fail her publishers or her audience. In *Lark Ascending* the Whiteoaks were temporarily abandoned, but she continued the tradition of presenting passionate, strong-willed characters caught in various love poses. She obviously hoped that her romantic characters gamboling about romantic Sicily would also enthrall the legion of Whiteoak fans. This new Play of Miss de la Roche was undoubtedly based on two trips in 1929 and 1931 to Taormina. In 1929, she and Miss Clement were seeing Europe for the first time; and in Taormina, where they stayed for eleven weeks, they were much involved in English society teas and private theatricals. Though they were much attracted by the beauty of the countryside and the colorful life of the Sicilians, they were plagued by too much sun (Miss de la Roche was sunblinded, and both ladies suffered severe sunburn) and then cold rain. Also, Miss de la Roche complained in a letter, printed by Ronald Hambleton, of the high cost of living in Sicily (122-24). In her autobiography, she is extremely hesitant about her experiences in Sicily and Italy (perhaps because it was there that she met the parents of the children she later adopted). About the 1931 trip and the resulting fiction, she says offhandedly:

. . .I had in mind to begin a new novel, something quite different from the Whiteoaks novels—for I thought I had done with them when *Finch's Fortune* was finished. The scene of this new novel was to open in New England, then move on to Sicily. When I told Ellery Sedgwick of this he implored me to stick to the country I knew—to write of Canada, not of New England. But I persisted, and when he read the completed manuscript he said he very much liked it (223-24).

The 1931 trip, one learns from a letter of February 15, 1931, to Katherine Hale (published by Mr. Hambleton), had provided much additional colorful background material. Miss de la

Roche recalled seeing an Italian carnival, which was unfortunately wrecked by cold wind. She continued, rather gushingly: "There were all sorts of floats carrying figures, some beautiful, some grotesque. The air was full of confetti and laughter. Little donkeys were covered with Ribbands and tassels. I do love the gaiety of the Italians. And they have so much to be sad for! And they work so hard. . ." (132).

The local color of the carnival was worked into the novel, but Miss de la Roche's primary concern was showing the clash of American and European cultures. She was trying to write an International Novel. To find that she failed is hardly surprising.

She was an expatriate for ten years; and, had she kept on working on serious themes instead of the hermetically sealed world of the Whiteoaks, she might have written an International Novel of value. The novel she did write, however, had several interesting themes, though they were never explored and were largely covered over with romantic claptrap.

The first sixty-nine pages of *Lark Ascending* were set in Massachusetts. The *ménage à trois* was made up of Fay Palmas, recently widowed owner of a family bakery, who was in love with her son and was obsessed with the idea of developing her lost voice; her young relative, Josie Froward, who worked in the family bakery and was in love with Fay's son Diego; and Diego, the indolent young painter, who was in love with himself. The outsider wanting inside was Purlie Bond, town druggist, who wanted to marry Fay.

In the tradition of the Play and bad popular fiction in all parts of the world, the practical difficulties of these four rather odd people, the problems of selling bakery and drug store to raise money for passage and living expenses in Europe were glossed over.

> "If only someone will come along and buy us out!" Fay cried.
> [Next sentence]: Someone did. Before the New Year, both the drug store and the bakery had been disposed of and their passages were booked on a foreign cruiser (69).

An English professor might boggle at the idea of a drug store and bakery, hand in hand, no doubt, taking a foreign cruise, but such gaucheries did not bother devoted fans.

Housewives from Vancouver to Glasgow were to believe, wanted to believe, needed to believe that it was possible for a woman like Fay (like themselves) to abandon a life of toil and suddenly become a world traveler. And they were also to believe that at Tenerife, when the other members of her party were ashore, Fay looked over the side of the ship and saw in a small boat a handsome young man: "She noticed the slender elegance of his body—he was bare to the waist—his cameo-like, Grecian features, his long bronze hair" (81). She was enthralled in the same way audiences were when Clark Gable revealed his chest, without undershirt, in *It Happened One Night*.

Not only was Fay attracted by his body, but she also discovered he was Count Montleone. Ladies in Minneapolis who had been washing dishes only an hour before were to tingle with anticipation of scenes to follow—and the expected scenes were written. Fay gave her beautiful count money, and she changed the travel plans of her whole party: they would not go to France; they would instead go to Sicily, his home.

In Naples, Diego became infatuated with Varvara, the Russian mistress of an Englishman; and, since the girl was bored with her current lover, she was readily convinced to appear also in Sicily. In Tramontana (as Miss de la Roche fictionalized it) Fay discovered that, though her count had lost the family mansion, he still owned the furniture. Fay was still enamored with his body and his Continental manners; they were married and decided to live by renting the mansion, opening an antique shop, and selling ancestral furniture and other pieces bought in the neighborhood. Josie was to open a "tea shoppe" for the tourists. Purlie refinished the furniture. Diego went his own way, that is to say he spent almost all of his time with Varvara, who tried constantly to seduce him—but this was Playland fiction, and the two were not lovers! Ladies back in Montana had been able to tell from the first that Varvara was a "bad woman" and not "right" for Diego.

The antique shop was a great success; Josie's "tea shoppe" was a great success. Fay was a countess; Josie was cousin of a countess. The sun shone at all times; no cold winds ruined the carnival. Ah, it was romantic and colorful; of course, Purlie pined for Fay, and Josie still loved Diego; but such problems are the very stuff of fiction for women. Then the count took to gambling and failed to bank the receipts from the antique sales. Fay raged, but she was satisfied by her Latin lover, and he was forgiven. But how was the rent to be paid?

The gods were in the wings, and the gods ignored depression America and sent down a rich American businessman who had previously bought furniture from the count and countess. The businessman was drawn to Purlie, who mixed medicines for the ailing stomach of the merchant. Suddenly the reader discovers that Purlie knew how to make a fine face cream, and the businessman bought the formula to produce the cream and market it in America. The advertisement which appeared in American journals was one of Miss de la Roche's attempts at a comedy of manners. Beneath a picture of Fay was this caption: "the beautiful Contessa Montleone, leader of one of Italy's most patrician circles, in whom is blended the regal dignity of the old noblesse with the exquisite graciousness of the modern society woman, attributes the fragrant delicacy of her skin . . . to the constant use of Bond's Face Cream" (266). Nothing more was made of commercialism or advertising.

Miss de la Roche hastened on to another theme: Russian artists had bitterly attacked Josie for completing Diego's paintings, calling her action "the touch of death." The scene was a forced one between the sophisticated Russian artists and the intuitive artist Josie, and one might speculate that Miss de la Roche was exploring Miss Clement's constant involvement in the fiction of her adopted sister. But the problem was not illuminated: Josie simply quit finishing the paintings, and the theme was dropped. The problem of Fay's lost voice was re-introduced (Miss de la Roche, one remembers, had periods when she could not write), but nothing was made of the artist's agony over a diminishing or interrupted talent. These serious themes on the nature of art were merely introduced and then permitted to die.

Miss de la Roche was more interested in a grand finale. Purlie had lent money to the countess to buy the ancestral home. The count, however, had become a wastrel. (Ladies in Dallas had long suspected such Latin types.) Fay caught him passionately kissing Varvara, and melodramatically terminated their marriage. (Thirty years later, the indiscretion would have been more explicit, but the scene is enough to suggest that *something* had already happened before Fay caught them.) Montleone tried to appease his wife, but Varvara was explicit. She was bored with Diego, who, after all, wouldn't sleep with her. She and the count, she explained, were Europeans; and then she *stated* the international theme of the novel:

"You are many centuries behind us. It is only for us to tolerate you while we must—while there is nothing better . . . . You have much to make up for what you lack. Your strength—your newness—your aggressiveness . . . . See, you have taken all that Montleone had—his house—his garden—his name . . . . He has nothing left but his spirit, his knowledge, come down to him from Romans and Greeks and Saracens and Moors. You cannot take that. You cannot understand that" (278-79).

This theme was never effectively dramatized, only baldly stated.

Then Miss de la Roche hurried through to a conclusion. Josie and Purlie decided to marry and return to America. Fay remained after her husband had departed with his mistress, for she enjoyed playing at being a countess. In the ending, though it is somewhat sentimental, Miss de la Roche seems finally to have viewed objectively the dangers of living in a dream world, in spending one's life in a Play. Two years after Fay's husband had departed, two librarians from Massachusetts approached the contessa, asking the way to their pension. She admitted to knowing a few words of English and gave them directions. When she stopped at her gate, with the antique sign, she explained, "We of the old families are obliged to sell some of our cherished belongings in order to live." The librarians grieved for her and thought her tragic. One said, "If only we could know what her life has been!" (301).

As *The New York Times* reviewer noted on August 14, 1932, *Lark Ascending* is a "cheerful book" which lacks depth and craft. One must conclude that the characters are not motivated and that the many serious and frivolous themes are introduced and never really examined. Miss de la Roche could have moulded this material into an international comedy of manners, but the melodrama of the adolescent Play made this impossible. In truth, Miss de la Roche had a sense of humor but rarely a sense of comedy.

The plot of *Lark Ascending* has been given in such detail to demonstrate just how great was Miss de la Roche's effort and how huge her failure. The story must be relegated to the merely ludicrous, and, since much of the fiction that follows is of no higher quality, it will be treated more succinctly.

II *Fiction:* Growth of a Man

Growth of a Man (1938), written in England, was Miss de la Roche's attempt to write a *Bildungsroman.* Although she was fond of the novel, and she reported in her memoirs that her Boston publisher, Alfred McIntyre, preferred it to all her other novels, it too was not the success for which she hoped. Sensitive to the reading tastes of the public, she said in her autobiography, "not only were those who read it and liked it fewer than the readers of the *Whiteoak Chronicles* but it did not inspire in them the warmth, the affection, felt by many for the family at Jalna. I think it lacks the warmth and humour" (279).

The most interesting part of the novel was the early life of Shaw Manifold on a Canadian farm. Although the story of agricultural hardships was done much better by Hamlin Garland, Miss de la Roche did manage to suggest the drudgery and tediousness of farm life. Shaw, in fact, decided to escape through education; and the author then added great touches of local color about Canadian rural schools. Hanging over Shaw's life, however, was the scourge of tuberculosis: his father had died from it, and his mother feared her son would develop it, as indeed he did.

After Shaw completed school, he went away to study forestry; and this section of the novel was a complete failure. Miss de la Roche, who had lived on a farm at one time and who knew something of that life, obviously knew next to nothing about life at an agricultural college. She then moved her hero to the Canadian West to survey forests there; she tried to suggest the sweep of Canada and the greatness of its natural resources. The descriptions were, however, too much those of a guidebook to be of interest. It is clear that Miss de la Roche knew far too little about what she was writing.

At the end of Shaw's studies in western Canada, he went to the United States to continue the study of forestry. He took a walking tour through South Carolina and Georgia, but he became ill, supposedly of malaria. If Miss de la Roche was at a

loss in describing the Canadian West, she was worse than amateurish in describing the American South. As the novel progressed, it became clear that she was wise in retreating to the
fantasy of Jalnaland, instead of attempting to deal with the
toads and the gardens in the real world.

On another trip West, Shaw became lost in a snowstorm, almost froze, contracted pneumonia, and then the dreaded tuberculosis. For three years he underwent treatment. After his
cure, he married and took his mother and wife to the Canadian
West where he was to be Head of the Department of Forestry.
As the novel ended, he was thinking of giving up his government job for a partnership in the lumber business, where, of
course, he would not rape the forests!

Apart from the farm scenes, the novel is not realistic and is
certainly too sketchy. The ending trails off into nothingness.
Perhaps Miss de la Roche, anticipating another success, thought
of unfolding another series about Shaw Manifold.

III *Fiction:* The Two Saplings

The Two Saplings (1942) is a thesis-ridden discussion of he-
redity and environment with a tacked-on patriotic ending. The
novel was obviously written to appeal to readers in wartime
England and America. It was published in England, but Miss de
la Roche's American publishers refused to publish it.[1] The story began with one of those coincidences overworked by writers
of novels and of film, radio, and television scripts: in a nursing
home in London, a nurse confused the only two babies in the
nursery. An American couple, the Wildes (Miss de la Roche
showed her view of Americans in the name selected), took the
baby of the Rendels, an English couple. Several years later,
when the boys were teen-agers, the Wildes and Rendels met on a
ship; and the parents began to unravel the mysteries of the
exchanged children. The parents, without telling the children
why, decided to switch children for a year. These scenes were
overly emotional and much drawn out and demonstrated perfectly that Miss de la Roche could have been Queen of the
Soap Opera Writers had she so desired.

The following complications were exactly what one would
expect. The American boy was introduced to hazing in the Eng-

lish prep school. The English boy, newly come to America, was more interested in news about England's involvement in World War II than in having his teeth straightened. Mrs. Wilde decided not to tell her son who he was. In a set piece, she told her husband, in language found only in novels: ". . . he belonged to the Rendels—not to us. To England—not to America. They have made him what he is. It would be terribly cruel to uproot him . . . I saw, too, that parenthood can't be shared. Children are either yours or they aren't. Sharing them would kill something in them that is their right" (212-13).

The American boy returned just before the English boy was ready to go back to a wartime England. When the Wildes saw the two boys on a large rock on the lawn, Mr. Wilde said, expressing a sentiment in hundreds of World War II movies and novels: "Their sort—the American and the Englishman—will have to build a new world when this war is over. And I must say, they look well fitted for the job."

The novel is a complete failure. The characters have the same depth as comic-strip or soap-opera characters, and the ending was obviously added for the benefit of Gold Star Mothers everywhere in the Anglo-Saxon world. A certain kind of reader in wartime England, however, wanted to read just such a book. The Macmillan clipping book in London contains twenty-five reviews and notices. The *Western Mail*, in Perth, for April 29, 1943, said in a typical review: "It is a book which can be read in a few hours . . . it has no deep plot, no climax, but it presents an interesting problem in an interesting manner and paints a background of both English and American life in the vivid colours which readers have come to associate with the author's works."

IV   *Short Stories:* A Boy in the House and Other Stories *and* The Sacred Bullock and Other Stories of Animals

The short stories in *A Boy in the House and Other Stories* (1952) were meant for a popular audience. Many of them appeared in *Harper's Bazaar* (London), *Good Housekeeping* (London), and *The Canadian Home Journal*. Two examples suffice to indicate the subject matter and approach, which were obviously intended to reach a particular type of feminine reader.

In "Auntimay" May Baxter had devoted her life to her family, first her parents, then her brother, then his three children. When the children were grown, she had no more responsibilities and shocked her proper middle-class relatives by becoming a clothes model in an expensive restaurant. What bored middle-class woman could fail to identify with May and dream of escaping her own narrow existence as she read the story? May met a distinguished gentleman who had her model several gowns, saying they were for his wife. The two were attracted to each other; he soon reported his wife had died. May learned later that he had never been married. May married her Mr. Wycherley, secured freedom and wealth, but missed having a family dependent upon her. While out for a drive, she saw her niece with a baby and learned the girl had been abandoned. May moved the girl and tiny daughter into her house. The moral is pervasive: everything will always come out right for the Mays of the world who devotedly do their duty.

"The Submissive Wife" was an anecdote about a compliant wife, married to a boor. At a Riviera hotel, she met a writer, and they ran away to England. She was miserable there, away from sun and tropical fruit. Her husband died; she could then marry the writer; and they could honeymoon on the Riviera. The story was completely without substance and was meant to entertain ladies on foggy afternoons; to let them dream of shedding their own boorish husbands and of escaping to the romantic Riviera.

The last story in the collection—"A Boy in the House"—was almost a success. The setting was obviously the house the Roches moved to after they were forced to leave the fruit farm in Bronte. One of the central characters was a writer named Lindley who wanted a secluded place to write. He had taken part of a house belonging to two eccentric sisters, Mrs. Morton and Miss Dove. They were impoverished, and the grounds around their house were overgrown. To help them cope, Mrs. Morton decided to get a boy from an orphanage to live with them; she brought home Eddy, a thirteen-year-old crippled boy who had been mistreated by parents and foster parents.

Lindley was fascinated by the boy and his movements, by

"the charming proportions of his slender body," and thought of him as aristocratic. When Eddy came to the writer's apartment to ask if Mrs. Morton's piano playing was bothersome, Lindley, who kept looking at him, yearned to "touch him, to find out if this fascination the boy had for him would vanish at the touch, but he refrained" (183). In the background, Mrs. Morton played romantic music.

The sisters began to have terrible quarrels and Eddy kept the arguments going. Lindley's book progressed, and one hot night, while taking a walk, he saw Eddy and neighborhood children taking a swim without clothes. As he watched, he saw them play like young animals. Lindley's eyes kept resting "on Eddy's agile little body" (197). During the hot summer, the two ladies became more quarrelsome. Eddy, burning with a high fever, saw Mrs. Morton fatally stab Miss Dove; and he was prevailed upon by Mrs. Morton to take the blame for the murder. He was sentenced to the reformatory until he was eighteen. Lindley, meanwhile, went on living in the apartment and completed his book. He then went to the reformatory, where the superintendent reported Eddy had a fine voice. Lindley decided he would have Eddy's voice trained. Even if the voice is worthless, he thought, Eddy is not worthless—"not with that look in his eyes —not after what he had done for Mrs. Morton" (243).

Underneath the melodramatic murder is a story of homosexual passion. The overgrown garden, the rotting fruit on the trees, the growing passion of the writer for the boy are all significant parts of a story Miss de la Roche does not know how to present. The nonsexual motives of Lindley, Eddy, Mrs. Morton, and Miss Dove are never clear. Curiously enough, Miss de la Roche included the story in a volume intended for pleasant reading for pleasant ladies. Perhaps she did not understand the central theme of her story, though at times the forbidden passion of Lindley appears to have a private meaning for her. When reading Miss de la Roche, one can never quite tell just how far her awareness extended.

An earlier collection, *The Sacred Bullock and Other Stories of Animals* (1939), did not contain any story of merit. In "Justice for an Aristocrat," for example, a horse was court-martialed and shot after the Russian Revolution because he was an aristocrat and had won a silver cup awarded by the Czar. Many of the stories were sentimental accounts of domestic pets. The amateurish stories are interesting only as they show the reading habits of many English and American women during the 1930's.

V *Biographies of Her Children:* Beside a Norman Tower
and
The Very House

Beside a Norman Tower (1934) is an account of Miss de la Roche's young adopted children, called Diggory and Gillian. Her aim, as stated in the introduction, is highly laudable:

The books about children which I have read are always concerned with those of five years or more, when they have been urged, moulded, dragged into some semblance of adults. I have asked myself if it is possible to write an interesting book about those mysterious beings who live in a grand tempestuous world of their own into which we can no more than enviously peer. This story of two toddlers is an attempt to answer that question.

Unfortunately Miss de la Roche did not peer deeply into the world of early childhood. What she did write was an episodic account of certain scenes in which the children appear as rather pert actors. There is no controlling point of view; there is no entry into the minds of the children; there is, instead, a series of "cute" stories; as a result the book is an inane failure. In her memoirs, Miss de la Roche states her reason for writing the book and, unwittingly, perhaps, helps to explain its failure: "It was necessary for me to have a respite from the exacting Whiteoaks. Yet write I must" (235). The material itself was, as she admits, the jottings of a "doting parent" who "made note of . . . infant doings."

Ronald Hambleton argues that the study succeeds because Miss de la Roche was experimenting with time. In her attempt to suggest the timeless world of the young child, he argues, she utilized present tense throughout. It is this suspension of time, not the sayings of children, he argues, which leads the reader to experience the scene (199). Mr. Hambleton's argument is ingenious, but one need only compare Miss de la Roche's account of the childhood of her two children with Faulkner's imaginative childhood scenes in *Sound and the Fury* to see how romantic Miss de la Roche's is.

Miss de la Roche continued the biography of the children in *The Very House* (1937). The second installment was comparable to the first, but reviewers liked both volumes. Grace Adams in *Books,* December 16, 1934, commended Miss de la Roche for the realistic writing in *Beside a Norman Tower. The Times Literary Supplement* review for October 16, 1937, of *The Very House* praised the universality of the story: "The infant hero and heroine become enchanting to a larger public than their mother, nurse and faithful chronicler" (756).

Both stories are important in understanding the paradoxical spinsters, Miss de la Roche and Miss Clement, who clearly loved the children as if they were their own. The two stories, however, have biographical, not literary, interest.

VI   *Miss de la Roche as Historian:* Quebec: Historic Seaport

Miss de la Roche's *Quebec: Historic Seaport,* published in 1944, was clearly the work of an amateur. No footnotes and no bibliography mar her study, but she did mention that her greatest indebtednesses were to previous histories by Francis Parkman and George Wrong. When a popular novelist writes popular history, one can expect picturesque details; and Miss de la Roche did not ignore them. She did note that *Quebec* would be her one history. And, she said ". . . with mingled audacity and apprehension, I deposit this cuckoo's egg in the austere nest of the historians" (viii).

Critical response to *Quebec* was limited. Catherine McKenzie, for example, in *The New York Times* for July 30, 1944, wrote an analysis which is fair and does not need to be amplified: "Because the author of the 'Jalna' series wrote this story of Quebec it will be read by many people who would never open Parkman. It is not fair to complain that the author does not write in that historian's clear, vivid prose, or even to complain of a florid confusion of style, with its fluttering references to 'beautiful French ladies,' in which the author's admirers may find pleasure . . . . the chief merit of this book is the impatient speed with which its hothouse artificialities sends one back to the refreshing vigor of the Jesuit Relations" (10).

VII *Miss de la Roche's Stories for Children*

In the 1950's, Miss de la Roche published two small books for children. Both were tastefully designed and well illustrated, but the stories were rather too saccharine, even for small children. In the first—*The Song of Lambert* (1955)—Lambert the Lamb could sing, but he was sold to make cutlets for Mr. van Grunt, a rich American businessman with poor digestion. Mr. van Grunt, an unhappy capitalist on his way to the South Pole, learned Lambert could sing and spared him. Soon the lamb was reunited with his family. A small child might well believe in a singing lamb or vegetarianism, but he might have difficulty accepting the caricature of the businessman or even the happy ending. Children know that lambs sold to butchers do become cutlets, not pampered baritones.

Bill and Coo (1958), despite all the niceties of bookmaking, was even sillier. Bill and Coo's first babies were drowned in a great storm, but Coo refused to leave the nest, even though the Dullards who owned the house where they had built their nest hated pigeons and would not feed them during the long winter. The next spring, their mystic egg contained a seraph, not a pigeon. The next door robins no longer were enemies, and the Dullards became friendly landlords bringing delicacies to the Angel, who finally ascended. In this instance, Miss de la Roche could not escape her simplified view of human and seraph nature. Children might indeed have difficulty in believing in the mysterious ways of the God of Bill and Coo and the Dullards, a god who sends a seraph into a bird's nest!

VIII *Miss de la Roche as Animal Lover:* Portrait of a Dog

Portrait of a Dog (1930) was a coy account of Bunty, a Christmas present from Miss de la Roche to her father, the last Christmas present she was to give him. No names were used in this account, the dog was always referred to as "you"; father, "he"; and Caroline, "the other one." The tone was that of an adoring mother: "That tail! Was there ever such another? A man, they say, may wear his heart on his sleeve; certainly you wore yours on your tail" (8). Miss de la Roche did avoid one pitfall; she did not portray the mind of the dog: "To me it seems that an impenetrable veil hangs between us and them [animals], that love them as we may we can never really understand their swift emotions, their wild and fleeting passions, and their loyalties. What does the world look like through their eyes? What monstrous shapes loom above them! What strange scents, howling terrors, bewildering joys and lusts sweep along the passionate course of their short lives!" (13).

In one section Miss de la Roche described the house which provided the setting for *A Boy in the House*. It was to this house that Bunty was brought: "The house was a strange one, part of it very old and weather-beaten . . . the other part a much later addition, always called by the owners 'the new wing', though it must have been fifty years old . . . . I thought of the two parts as two people united by a hateful bond, never having even pretended to care for each other" (19). The house clearly called forth deep and private meanings, but Miss de la Roche in this story of her dog and later in *A Boy in the House* was never able to make clear the great significance of the divided house and the divided sisters.

Miss de la Roche went through the entire life of the dog. It was a sentimental account but much admired by her fans, many of whom sent her pictures of their favorite dogs. The memoir obviously appealed to a great army of dog lovers.

IX *Miss de la Roche as Autobiographer:* Ringing the Changes

Ringing the Changes: An Autobiography (1957) was one of those peculiar Victorian-flavored documents which tell more and less than the author intended. The most intriguing sections of the memoirs dealt with the Play. In 1956, after she had completed *Ringing the Changes*, Miss de la Roche wrote Lovat Dickson (the letter is quoted by Hambleton): "It was a strange experience indeed to write this book, to prepare for the appearance in cold print of things which I had never talked of to anyone—for one thing the Play in which Caroline and I for many years lost ourselves and, in a way, found ourselves" (114).

Except for the description of the Play and its meaning in her artistic life, the memoirs are extremely peculiar. Scenes are presented in such dramatic fashion that it is clear a novelist with a romantic imagination has improved upon them greatly. Most of the dramatized scenes are set in a timeless world, as if the author were perpetually fifteen; it is virtually impossible to date any happening described. In Victorian tradition, the description of the emotional bonds which existed between Miss de la Roche and Miss Clement and between Miss de la Roche and her father are presented in a naïve, girlish fashion. Did Miss de la Roche deliberately reject modern psychology; and, in doing so, did she not reveal more than she intended?

The description of her creative life is most unsatisfactory. If Miss de la Roche had worked out esthetic concepts, she was not able to formulate them when writing her memoirs. Her greatest skill was in telling stories for romantically-inclined readers, and esthetic views would perhaps have ruined this ability of hers. The blurb writer for the English edition of the memoirs asked the rhetorical question: "In this long family chronicle stretching from generation to generation [of the Whiteoaks], has she been telling us something of herself?" English and American ladies must have been disappointed as they attempted to find the answer to this question.

The Times Literary Supplement reviewer on May 17, 1957, discussed her restless moves from house to house and from Canada to England and back to Canada. He wrote that she "has used up in fiction the impressions made upon her by her moves and travels and has little left over, whereas the deeper impressions of childhood can be returned to again and again without being exhausted." The reviewer pointed out that she had neither style, feeling, nor "the ability to convey atmosphere" but that her millions of readers obviously did not feel these lacks were defects (307). In similar tone *The Manchester Guardian* for June 18, 1957, said, "the one story she cannot tell is that of her own life." *The Catholic World* wickedly suggested the memoirs might better have been called, "Safe and Sound; or Out of Harm's Way."

To the very end of her career, her readers wanted only the family chronicles of the Whiteoaks, not any other fiction, not even her own story. In this respect, Miss de la Roche, like Conan Doyle, was held captive by adoring fans who wanted only the old familiar characters.

CHAPTER 6

Conclusion

A BRITISH publisher has correctly observed that Miss de la Roche "has been a gold mine to anyone who has ever had anything to do with her."[1] After her death, the Macmillan Company estimated that nine million hard-cover copies of the Jalna series had been sold; the Pan paperback editions had sold over two million copies by 1964. Translations in paper, as well as hard covers, are widely sold in Germany, France, Sweden, and in many other European countries. Paperbound editions are not as numerous in the United States, but the Jalna novels are staples in American public and lending libraries.

Just how much income Miss de la Roche derived from her writing is not known, but Ronald Hambleton has noted that "her estate was valued for probate purposes at just under half a million dollars" (54). And one must remember that, after her success with *Jalna*, she lived for a decade in England, moving frequently from one large house to another, with a retinue of servants for herself, Miss Clement, and her adopted children. Quite obviously she spent large sums.

Miss de la Roche had the adulation of thousands if not millions of readers, but her fans wanted to read about the Whiteoaks and largely ignored her non-Jalna fiction. Her audience was perceptive: the Jalna stories (except for *Delight*) are certainly more entertaining than Miss de la Roche's other writings. She had no major themes, made no profound comments on the human condition. Even had she been capable of writing a novel with the depths and intensity of Dickens' *Great Expectations*, Emily Brontë's *Wuthering Heights*, or Joseph Conrad's *Heart of Darkness*, it is not clear that the housewives who formed the majority of her audience would have accepted such a story from her.

Miss de la Roche's romantic imagination was perfectly attuned to the need of housewives, in whatever part of the world, to find imaginative surrogates for their humdrum lives. Judged not as a realist, not as a social critic, but as a writer of escape fiction, Miss de la Roche was a tremendous success. Her family dramas with their many erotic scenes provided wives and mothers with escape and entertainment. Read and admired by millions, she was for thirty years Canada's best-known writer. She had an eye for the comic, a fertile imagination, and the natural ability to tell a story. She did not seem to regard herself as a major writer; had she been under such a delusion, her life and work would appear tragic. As it was, after the success of the Jalna stories, she had several years of happiness with Miss Clement, their dogs, her adopted children. She had devoted readers who wanted to read more Whiteoak novels and not her other fiction. Her readers showed their admiration and devotion in their letters to her. Her publishers—Knopf, Macmillan, Little, Brown, and Company—had great prestige. She may not have written works as critically acclaimed as the Brontës, Dickens, and Galsworthy, but she clearly gave much pleasure to millions of readers. Such an achievement is, in itself, significant. ·

Notes and References

As noted in the Acknowledgments, many of the footnote references are included in the text.

Preface

1. *Time*, October 27, 1967, p. 105.

Chapter One

1. *Twentieth Century Authors* (New York, 1942), pp. 367-68.
2. See especially Chapters 4 and 5.
3. Emily Brontë, *Wuthering Heights* (Boston, 1956), p. 30.
4. Mazo de la Roche, *Ringing the Changes* (London, 1957), p. xii.
5. *Ibid.*, p. 38.
6. Ronald Hambleton, *Mazo de la Roche of Jalna* (New York, 1966), p. 113.
7. Lawrence and E. M. Hanson, *The Four Brontës* (London, 1950), p. 17.
8. *Ibid.*, pp. 17-18.
9. E. C. Gaskell, *The Life of Charlotte Brontë* (London, 1857), I, 87.
10. *Ibid.*, I, 88.
11. Lawrence and E. M. Hanson, p. 23.
12. Hambleton, p. 84.
13. *Ibid.*, p. 80.
14. Dorothy Livesay, "The Making of Jalna: A Reminiscence," *Canadian Literature* 23 (Winter 1965), 29.

Chapter Two

1. Quoted in Frank Luther Mott, *A History of American Magazines* (Cambridge, 1957), IV, 611.
2. *Ibid.*, IV, 619.
3. See Hambleton, p. 170, for a summary of the Canadian reviews.

Chapter Three

1. For a history of the publication of *Jalna*, see Chapter II of Hambleton and Chapter 4 of this study.

2. See Hambleton, pp. 164-65.

3. *Ibid.*, p. 219.

4. For a discussion of public interest in a filmed version of Margaret Mitchell's *Gone With the Wind*, see Finis Farr, *Margaret Mitchell of Atlanta* (New York, 1965), Chapter X.

5. Quoted in Hambleton, p. 143.

6. *Ibid.*, p. 148.

7. *Ibid.*, p. 150.

8. *Ibid.*, p. 150.

Chapter Four

1. Quoted in Carl F. Klinck, ed., *Literary History of Canada* (Toronto, 1965), p. 671.

2. In the de la Roche Collection, University of Toronto Library.

Chapter Five

1. Hambleton, p. 161.

Conclusion

1. Hambleton, p. 53.

Selected Bibliography

PRIMARY SOURCES

I. Jalna Novels

The Building of Jalna. Boston: Little, Brown, 1944; London: Macmillan, 1945.

Centenary at Jalna. Boston: Little, Brown, 1958; London: Macmillan, 1958.

Finch's Fortune. Boston: Little, Brown, 1931; London: Macmillan, 1931.

Jalna. Boston: Little, Brown, 1927; London: Hodder and Stoughton, 1927; London: Macmillan, 1929.

Mary Wakefield. Boston: Little, Brown, 1949; London: Macmillan, 1949.

The Master of Jalna. Boston: Little, Brown, 1933; London: Macmillan, 1933.

Morning at Jalna. Boston: Little, Brown, 1960; London: Macmillan, 1960.

Renny's Daughter. Boston: Little, Brown, 1951; London: Macmillan, 1951.

Return to Jalna. Boston: Little, Brown, 1946; London: Macmillan, 1948.

Variable Winds at Jalna. Boston: Little, Brown, 1954; London: Macmillan, 1955.

Wakefield's Course. Boston: Little, Brown, 1941; London: Macmillan, 1942.

The Whiteoak Brothers, Jalna—1923. Boston: Little, Brown, 1953; London: Macmillan, 1954.

Whiteoak Harvest. Boston: Little, Brown, 1936; London: Macmillan, 1936.

Whiteoak Heritage. Boston: Little, Brown, 1940; London: Macmillan, 1940.

Whiteoaks of Jalna. Boston: Little, Brown, 1929; London: Macmillan, 1929.

Young Renny (Jalna—1906). Boston: Little, Brown, 1935; London: Macmillan, 1935.

Pan Books brought out the extremely popular paper edition in England, reprinting all sixteen of the novels. In early 1968, only four paperback editions of the Jalna novels were available in the United States; they are *Finch's Fortune, Jalna, Master of Jalna,* and *Whiteoaks of Jalna,* all published by Crest. No attempt is made in this bibliography to list all the reprints in the United States and England.

Ronald Hambleton in *Mazo de la Roche of Jalna* states that the Jalna novels have been translated into sixteen languages and that there have been pirated editions in Poland, Czechoslovakia, and Hungary (50-51). For a listing of translations, see *Index Translationum, V.* 1 (1932)—.

II. Non-Jalna Fiction

A Boy in the House and Other Stories. Boston: Little, Brown; London: Macmillan, 1952. Contents: "Auntimay," "The Celebration," "Twa Kings," "The Submissive Wife," "The Broken Fan," "Patient Miss Peel," "A Word for Coffey," "The Widow Cruse," "Quartet," "A Boy in the House."
Delight. New York: Macmillan, 1926.
Explorers of the Dawn. New York: Knopf; London: Cassell and Company, 1922. Contents: "Buried Treasure," "The Jilt," "Explorers of the Dawn," "A Merry Interlude," "Freedom," "D' Ye Ken John Peel?" "Granfa," "Noblesse Oblige," "The Cobbler and His Wife," "The New Day."
Growth of a Man. Boston: Little, Brown; London: Macmillan, 1938.
Lark Ascending. Boston: Little, Brown; London: Macmillan, 1932.
Possession. New York: Macmillan; London: Macmillan, 1923.
The Sacred Bullock and Other Stories of Animals. Boston: Little, Brown; London: Macmillan, 1939. Contents: "April Day," "Cat's Cruise," "Electric Storm," "Justice for an Aristocrat," "Ninth Life," "Peter: A Rock," "Reunion," "The Pony that Would Not Be Ridden," "The Sacred Bullock," "The She Gull."
The Thunder of New Wings. Boston: Little, Brown, 1932. The novel was serialized in *Chatelaine,* July, 1932-February, 1933.
The Two Saplings. London: Macmillan, 1942. [No American edition.]

III. Plays

Low Life and Other Plays. Boston: Little, Brown, 1929. Contents: *Low Life, Come True, The Return of the Emigrant.*
Whiteoaks: A Play. Boston: Little, Brown; London: Macmillan, 1936.

IV. Autobiography

Ringing the Changes: An Autobiography. Boston: Little, Brown; London: Macmillan, 1957.

V.   Biographies

Beside a Norman Tower. Boston: Little, Brown; London: Macmillan,
    1934. [Biographical sketches of her adopted children.]
Portrait of a Dog. Boston: Little, Brown; London: Macmillan, 1930.
    [Biography of Bunty.]
The Very House. Boston: Little, Brown; London: Macmillan, 1937.
    [More biographical sketches of her adopted children.]

VI.   History

Quebec: Historic Seaport. Garden City: Doubleday, 1944; London:
    Macmillan, 1946.

VII.   Books for Children

Bill and Coo. Toronto: Macmillan; London: Macmillan, 1958.
The Song of Lambert. Boston: Little, Brown; London; Macmillan,
    1955.

VIII.   Uncollected and Unpublished Writings

Three uncollected stories are discussed in Chapter 2:
    "The Son of a Miser: How Noel Carron, of St. Loo, Proved That
    He Was No Pinchpenny," *Munsey's Magazine* (August, 1903), pp.
    750-57.
    "The Spirit of the Dance," *The Canadian Magazine* (May, 1910),
    pp. 37-48.
    "The Thief of St. Loo: An Incident in the Life of Antoine O'Neil,
    Honest Man," *Munsey's Magazine* (November, 1902), pp. 182-87.

    For a listing of uncollected and unpublished writings of Miss de
la Roche, see the bibliography in Hambleton's biography. A large number of manuscripts of Miss de la Roche's published and unpublished
works are now in the Department of Rare Books and Special Collections of the University of Toronto Library.

SECONDARY SOURCES

I.   Bibliographies

HAMBLETON, RONALD. *Mazo de la Roche of Jalna*. New York: Haw-
    thorn Books, 1966. Especially useful for its listing of short sto-
    ries published singly; for information on first publication of

stories in *Explorers of the Dawn, A Boy in the House and Other Stories,* and *The Sacred Bullock and Other Stories of Animals;* and for its listing of unpublished plays, short stories, and poems.

WATTERS, REGINALD EYRE. *A Check List of Canadian Literature and Background Materials 1628-1950,* Toronto: University of Toronto Press, 1959, pp. 197-98, 307, 449, 681. Bibliographical information on Miss de la Roche's publications and location of books in Canadian and American libraries.

————— and Inglis Freeman Bell. On *Canadian Literature 1806-1960.* Toronto: University of Toronto Press, 1966, pp. 89-90. Listing of articles on Miss de la Roche.

II.   Selected Criticism

DANIELLS, ROY. "Poetry and the Novel," *The Culture of Contemporary Canada.* Ithaca: Cornell University Press, 1957. Argues that the Whiteoaks are "fabrications of a lively fancy" and that Canadian critics have not understood what Miss de la Roche was about. The Jalna books are for export.

EAYRS, HUGH. "Mazo de la Roche." *Bookman* (October-November, 1938) pp. 17-22. Extravagant praise of Miss de la Roche: " . . . her genius not merely for character drawings but also for fitting them into the most perfect mosaic makes reading her books an unforgettable experience."

FARR, FINIS. *Margaret Mitchell of Atlanta.* New York: William Morrow, 1965. A useful account of a Popular Woman Novelist who wisely refrained from writing sequels.

GASKELL, ELIZABETH C. *The Life of Charlotte Brontë.* London: Smith, Elder and Co., 1857. 2 volumes. Useful for its discussions of the imaginary world of the Brontës and for understanding the Playland of Miss de la Roche and Miss Clement.

HACKETT, ALICE PAYNE. *60 Years of Best Sellers.* New York: Bowker, 1956. In 1927, when *Elmer Gantry* was first on the best-seller list, *Jalna* was fifth. Provides excellent source material for speculation on public taste.

HAMBLETON, RONALD. *Mazo de la Roche of Jalna.* New York: Hawthorn Books, 1966. Indispensable for its biographical information. For a Canadian reaction to this work, see Dorothy Livesay's review in *Canadian Literature,* No. 32 (Spring, 1967), 57-59.

HANSON, LAWRENCE and E. M. *The Four Brontës.* London: Oxford University Press, 1949. Synthesis of earlier Brontë studies. Should be read along with Mrs. Gaskell's biography of Charlotte and with Miss Ratchford's studies of the Brontës' juvenilia.

HART, JAMES D. *The Popular Book: A History of America's Literary*

Taste. New York: Oxford University Press, 1950. A standard study.

LEAVIS, Q. D. *Fiction and the Reading Public*. London: Chatto and Windus, 1932. Among other things, shows "that the general reading public of the twentieth century is no longer in touch with the best literature of its own day" and supplies some speculation on *why*.

Literary History of Canada: Canadian Literature in English. Carl F. Klinck, General Editor. Toronto: University of Toronto Press, 1965. Important reference work for the student of Canadian literature.

LIVESAY, DOROTHY. "The Making of Jalna: A Reminiscence," *Canadian Literature*, Number 23 (Winter 1965), 25-30. The Livesay family had a house near Trail Cottage. Miss Livesay's memoir of Miss de la Roche is appreciative; the conclusion, however, is that the Whiteoaks became sentimentalized and that Miss de la Roche had "no *point of view* in her writing."

MOTT, FRANK LUTHER. *Golden Multitudes: The Story of Best Sellers in the United States*. New York: Macmillan, 1947. The chapters "Is There A Best Seller Formula?" and "What Makes A Best Seller Sell?" are particularly useful to those studying modern popular fiction.

———. *A History of American Magazines*. Cambridge: Harvard University Press, 1938-1957. Vol. 4 contains a history of *Munsey's Magazine*, where Miss de la Roche published her St. Loo stories.

PACEY, DESMOND. "Fiction 1920-1940," in *Literary History of Canada*. Toronto: University of Toronto Press, 1965, pp. 669-72. Discusses with perception Miss de la Roche's fiction.

RATCHFORD, FANNIE ELIZABETH. *The Brontës' Web of Childhood*. New York: Columbia University Press, 1941.

———. *Legends of Angria*. New Haven: Yale University Press, 1933. Scholarly accounts of the childhood writings of the Brontës.

STORY, NORAH. *The Oxford Companion to Canadian History and Literature*. New York: Oxford University Press, 1967. "In *Possession* Mazo de la Roche first used a great house as the centre of a world . . . but the characters are weak. Later, when she matched the stature of the owner to that of the house, she found material for a family saga that captured a large and literate public at home and abroad" (206-207).

THURBER, JAMES. "Soapland," *The Beast in Me*. New York: Harcourt, Brace, 1948, pp. 191-260. Splendid account of the radio serial as a cultural phenomenon.

Twentieth Century Authors: A Biographical Dictionary of Modern Literature. Edited by Stanley J. Kunitz and Howard Haycraft.

New York: The H. W. Wilson Co., 1942. The biographical information on Miss de la Roche is sketchy and somewhat suspect. Criticizing the novels, the editors say that the Jalna novels "are not great or even major novels, but they have body and texture and life; they are full-blooded, and we read them with the same absorbed interest we give to the life-stories of people we know."

———. First Supplement. New York: The H. W. Wilson Co., 1955. Adds later publications of Miss de la Roche. The thesis of the sketch: "Few institutions in twentieth century life are more solid and permanent than the Whiteoak family."

WEEKS, EDWARD. *In Friendly Candor.* Boston: Little, Brown, 1959. Contains a restrained essay on Miss de la Roche. The unpleasant aspects of the author-editor relationship of the two are not explored.

WELLAND, D. S. R. "Hemingway's English Reputation," *The Literary Reputation of Hemingway in Europe.* Ed. by Roger Asselineau. New York: New York University Press, 1965. The British Book Society Committee chose *Whiteoaks of Jalna* over *A Farewell to Arms* because, as J. B. Priestley explained, " 'A Farewell to Arms,' far rougher and more outspoken, a brutally masculine performance, is not everybody's book" (p. 19).

WILSON, EDMUND. "O Canada: An American's Notes on Canadian Culture," in *The New Yorker,* November 14, 21, 28, 1964. Also published under the same title by Farrar, Straus and Giroux, 1965. Useful notes on Canadian culture. No direct comments on Miss de la Roche.

NOTE: Newspaper and magazine reviews of Miss de la Roche's books are not listed here, but citations are given in the text. The Clipping Book of de la Roche reviews in the London office of Macmillan was of great benefit in finding reviews, as was *Book Review Digest* from 1927 to 1960.

Index